My Head for a Tree

The Extraordinary Story of the Bishnoi, the World's First Eco-Warriors

My Head for a Tree

The Extraordinary Story of the Bishnoi, the World's First Eco-Warriors

MARTIN GOODMAN

foreword by
PETER WOHLLEBEN

preface by
RAM NIWAS BISHNOI BUDHNAGAR

with photographs by
FRANCK VOGEL

Profile Books

Published in Great Britain in 2025 by

Profile Books
29 Cloth Fair, London ECIA 7JQ

www.profilebooks.com

1 3 5 7 9 10 8 6 4 2

Typeset in Garamond
to a design by Henry Iles.

A CIP catalogue record for this book is available from the
British Library.

ISBN 978-1800818712

Printed and bound in Great Britain by
CPI Group (UK) Ltd, Croydon CR0 4YY

For the Bishnoi, carers of our natural world,
who asked me to share their story

How can these be the right things to do? You have no fear of God but are ready to frighten others; you perform no good deeds of your own but expect others to do so; you say nothing that is kind and ask others to speak cruelly; you do not want to die but are happy to kill others. Practise before preaching. Make sure you do what needs be done before you die.

A tree covered in greenery is my temple and my home.

GURU JAMBHOJI

Contents

Preface

Ram Niwas Bishnoi Budhnagar

For a Bishnoi, caring for the natural world is a completely natural and traditional way of living. It is unimaginable not to do so. We learn it from our parents and our children learn it from us. It is a continuous process that is passed from one generation to another. Our children remember the last words of Amrita Devi, who sacrificed her life to protect the green trees three hundred years ago. We are always ready to give our lives to protect trees and animals, because they give us so much.

Our Guru Jambhoji taught us how to live in harmony with nature. He learned this lesson from the times of severe drought in the desert of Rajasthan. In that distant time, in the sixteenth century, he was a man who could see our future. The lessons from then apply globally to the current climate change emergency. We don't ask that people become Bishnois, but we know that many of you care deeply about our planet and the trees, plants and wildlife with which we share it. Please read this book, learn something about the Bishnoi, and see how we live our lives; it may help you live yours.

Author's note

The Bishnoi are 'probably the most ecologically conscious community in the world'.[1] Bishnoism is the one world religion that has environmental protection as its very core. Their founding guru, Jambhoji (1451–1536), is an equivalent of other religious founders such as Jesus, Buddha and Mohammed, only more recent. Born into a farming community in Rajasthan, he removed himself to a hilltop retreat and received a world-changing vision while in meditation beneath a tree. From this he delivered rules for living that guided desert people how to survive a fierce and enduring drought. They learned how to shift their way of life away from competing with the natural world and toward living in harmony with it.

In perhaps the bravest acts of nature conservation ever seen, Bishnois have redefined how humans should interact with the living world. Though they might not call it brave. Would a mother think of herself as brave for snatching her child out of the path of an onrushing truck? You do what your own nature calls you to do.

The story of the Bishnoi is one of those 'greatest stories never told'. Or at least very little told in English, and not that well known even in India.

So how come I was given the chance to write it?

I was at a festival in Jaipur to present a book I had written about eco-lawyers saving the planet. My life is something of a quest, and previous visits to India had led me to transformative experiences with spiritual leaders and sacred places. My new goal was to encounter people who dedicated their lives to protecting natural habitat. That's why a leading conservationist in India directed me toward the Bishnoi.

From a base in the city of Jodhpur, Bishnois guided me to their farms, their homes, their schools, their temples and animal shelters, and a village funeral. Perhaps, in retrospect, I was being vetted. Some elements were in place: I had written a book about people saving the planet, was out in the world to deliver its message, and was a university professor, eager to learn. You'll read in the coming chapters how this book was 'commissioned', before a large and receptive audience of Bishnois and in a way I could not refuse. The Bishnoi are doing their best to save the planet, but the current ecological crisis is dreadful and time is short, and the way of life they practise, the teachings given to them by their desert guru, shouldn't be secret. The West should know about them.

I am not a Bishnoi and can never become one. You can only be born a Bishnoi. I would never have presumed to write this story, but having been asked to do so, the best I can do is offer my Western perspective on a people who live more kindly on this planet.

The Bishnoi lead by example. We would do well to follow, as best we can.

Foreword

Peter Wohlleben

When I first heard about this book, I was electrified. There's a community in India who protect trees with their lives? How could it be that I'd never heard of the Bishnoi? These must be my brothers and sisters in spirit, I thought, whose environmental stance is similar to my own. As I continued to read the manuscript, I realised that the principles of the Bishnoi go much further and with far more consequences than my own. One of the key events in the history of this religion is a well-documented massacre – 300 years ago – of villagers who prevented the felling of their trees by hugging them. Today, tree hugging is seen more as an opportunity to connect with nature, to slow down, or to shift our regard of these gentle giants.

Modern nature conservation efforts suffer from the same problems that drive the overconsumption of industrial nations: we attach a price tag to every living thing to prevent it from being overlooked in our value system. Examples of such price tags include the amount of carbon dioxide trees contain, how much oxygen they produce, the measurable amount of cooling they can provide, and the impact on available fresh water. In other words, trees are deemed valuable in relation to their usefulness to us, and the associated monetary worth.

These aspects are undoubtedly important, also for the Bishnoi, and the monetisation of ecosystem services (what an unwieldy, technical term) has at least helped to curb the worst excesses of environmental degradation. However, what we are currently seeing is that conservation is often used as a political pawn, sacrificed at the altar of other interests. In Europe, the protection of our forests, indeed all protection of climate and the environment, is being hollowed out in an effort to leach support from right-wing parties. The truth is, unfortunately, that despite various partial international successes, environmental protection efforts are not improving. Market-based measures that are meant to constrain environmentally harmful lobby groups are obviously not working.

It is precisely at this point that the book begins, and it is precisely why its key message is so important: the protection of the environment, of trees and of animals must function at an emotional level; it must be an internalised necessity for every human. It is essential that the refusal to harm trees and other fellow creatures becomes a social norm. The Bishnoi embody this attitude in its purest form. They teach me humility – me, who sees himself as an ambassador for the trees but who has never considered going to such extremes. At the same time, the Bishnoi fuel my desire to dedicate my life to the protection of trees and forests.

What an enormous contribution Martin Goodman offers by bringing this culture and religion closer to us. This book, thrilling to the last page, fills a gap in the environmental debate. It can offer inspiration to many readers who wish to concentrate on the truly important things in life. We cannot all be Bishnoi. Indeed, one must be born into that culture to belong. But this book may help us to grow in our empathy and to do more for the trees in our forests, our streets and our gardens. This isn't about saving the trees so much as it is about saving ourselves, since the natural environment is a reflection of who we are.

Peter Wohlleben is the author of *The Hidden Life of Trees*. His foreword was translated from the German by B.L. Crook.

My Head for a Tree

...ARE SAVED IN EXCHANGE
IT WILL BE CHEAP TRANSACTION
"AMRITA DEVI BISHNOI"

TO SAVE TREES
...ISHNOI PEOPLE SACRIFICED THEIR LIVES IN 1730 AD IN VILLAG...

1

Amrita Devi and the 363 Martyrs

LET'S START WITH A TRUE STORY. The year is 1730. The village of Khejarli is in the Thar Desert, which sweeps through north-west India. Thirteen miles to the east lies the fortified city of Jodhpur where the Maharajah Abhay Singh was building himself a new palace.

In the early mornings the village people washed before pouring ghee on a sacred flame and chanting their prayers. Then the genders divided. The men gathered their flocks of goats and herds of cattle. Grass was sparse, growing in tufts among rocks and bare dirt. The men, white turbans around their heads and wearing white smocks and trousers, walked long circuits with their herds until the beasts had found their food.

The women's clothes blazed with the hues of fire; oranges and reds and yellows and pinks. It was the women who scrubbed and pounded and hung the men's clothes in the sun and kept them white. No white for them – it was the colour of mourning. The cattle's movement out of the village stirred the animals' guts; cow pats could still be steaming when the women took them into their hands. They moulded them into bricks of fuel and left them to bake in sunlight. Before lighting these cow pats for their fires the women ran their palms and fingers across the bumps of their surface, puffing gusts of air from their cheeks, blowing and brushing any insects to safety.

These were desert women who knew not to cut limbs from a living tree. The life in a tree is too precious. Any twigs on the fire had to be dead when found. One particular species of tree is foremost in holding the soil of this landscape in place: the khejri.

The thin branches of desert khejri are spiked with protective thorns. Its leaves are like the veins of a leaf without the green in between, tiny and feather-like and dark and waxy. They don't want their moisture to evaporate. Eventually they grow beyond the reach of a camel's lips and spread a canopy. Seen from afar those leaves could be a large cloud of insects. They cluster so thickly that camels rest in their shade.

A 'forest' of khejri sees the trees spaced out, offering places of shelter with their pools of shade. When the ground is monsoon-wet, villagers plant sapling khejri in the more open spaces. The trees form part of an ecosystem. They offer shelter to animals and their roots help hold the desert in place. Khejri are also leguminous, so those roots are fixing nitrogen into the soil and so encouraging crops to grow between the trees.

On Monday 11 September 1730 (although this reads like a fable the details are recorded, including the names of the people involved) the men of Khejarli were away with their herds. The monsoon rains were recent so a woman of the village, Amrita Devi, was tending the crops with her three daughters – Asu, Ratni and Bhagu. She lifted her head. She had heard men's voices. But it was too early, surely, for the village men to be returning with their herds. She heard creaks from wooden oxcarts and the thwacks of sticks on hide, shouts to goad oxen through mud.

Amrita rushed through the trees like a red flame. Men in the uniforms of the Maharajah's forces were pulling axes from the backs of the carts. One man was giving orders and Amrita stood herself in front of him.

The men had marched out from Jodhpur, she learned, where the Maharajah had plans for a new palace. Its construction needed lime, and for the lime they needed fire and to fuel the fire they needed trees. The men had come to chop down the khejri forest and haul it to the city to be burned.

This could not be allowed to happen.

Pay us a bribe, the officer suggested, though he called it a tax. A tax for every tree. And then the men would march off and chop down someone else's trees.

Amrita could no more pay a bribe than she could kill an animal or eat meat or herself harm a tree. Her life worked because she was a Bishnoi who lived by a clear set of twenty-nine rules set down by her guru more than two hundred years earlier, which saw accepting bribes to be as sinful as stealing. These rules governed her life. One was an injunction to protect all living beings. Another was not to cut trees that had the sap of life still in them. So she hugged her body close to a khejri tree, and as the men approached she spoke the words that children would learn and recite for generations to come: *Sar sāntey rūkh rahe to bhī sasto jān.* 'My head for a tree; it's a cheap price to pay.'

A man with an axe chopped off her head.

Amrita's three daughters, Asu, Ratni and Bhagu, watched their mother's sacrifice. They heard her last words. They saw the blade cut through her neck and her head fly free. They saw the fount of blood from her body. They were young.

Asu stepped forward to hug a tree.

As did Ratni.

As did Bhagu.

The axemen chopped off their heads.

Word of the attack went round the other Bishnoi villages. The old who didn't roam so far were the first to arrive and as they grabbed on to trees they too were beheaded. Then the news reached the men of Khejarli, who ran home ahead of their goats and their cattle, arriving into a massacre. They too held on to trees and gave their lives. Other Bishnoi walked in from nearby villages, grasped hold of a tree, and were chopped to death.

'You villagers,' the officer in charge of the Jodhpur troops scoffed, 'you're only sending in the old and the weak.'

In response, young men came, and women and more children. Each held on to a khejri tree, chanted holy mantras and the words of their guru, and gave their life.

A couple were passing, fresh from their wedding. What good was their life with all its hopes if they walked on past this killing of a forest? The bride and groom each took hold of a tree. Each was killed.

Word spread further still and people kept on coming. One hundred people. Two hundred people. Three hundred people. They gave their heads to save the trees. Word finally crossed the thirteen miles of desert to Jodhpur and the Maharajah.

Shocked by the news, the Maharajah ordered his men to withdraw. When the killing ended, three hundred and sixty-three villagers had been martyred. The Maharajah issued an edict: it was now forbidden to chop down a living tree, and to hunt or poach any animal, throughout Bishnoi land.

The martyrs of Khejarli were all Bishnois. They have a word, *sakasi*, for those who sacrifice their life for others. The first recorded *sakasi* came from 1604, a hundred and twenty-six years before the Khejarli massacre. In the village of Ramsari, near Jodhpur, two women called Karma and Gora were beheaded in defence of trees. Then in 1643, when trees were being felled for use in celebrations of the goddess Holi, a local Bishnoi named Buchoji killed himself in protest.

Are twenty-first-century Bishnois prepared to put their lives on the line to save trees? They are.

Would I die to save a child? I'd hope so.

Do I love trees? Yes.

Would I die for one? Not yet.

But who are these people who would?

2

One Morning with Cranes

WATCH OUT FOR THE BISHNOI. Giving your life to save a tree is one part of their character, but don't view it as being passive. See it as fierce. Attack what they hold dear and they'll come for you.

Ram Niwas is in his thirties, sturdy, watchful, his round face flicking disarming smiles. Watch out for those smiles. He's assessing. Waiting his moment.

Ram Niwas was fifteen when India's most famous man put on night-vision goggles and stole into a Bishnoi village. The man committed an outrage. Upset beyond belief, Ram Niwas joined a band set to wreak justice: the Bishnoi Tiger Force.

He grew up to be their leader.

We'll shortly learn the tale of Ram Niwas Bishnoi Budhnagar (most Bishnois carry Bishnoi as their surname, while a middle name denotes where they live: in Ram Niwas's case Budhnagar, the name of his home village).

Right now it's just past dawn on a January day and he has volunteered to be my guide into the Bishnoi world.

In 2021 Jodhpur absorbed 395 surrounding villages and so doubled in size to 2.3 million inhabitants. Ram Niwas drives us toward the city's village crust. He talks to his phone more than to me, in the local language Marwari and the related Hindi. My European languages leave me effectively mute, or as a child for whom words don't yet hold meaning. And indeed I've come because language has let me down. For Bishnois the tale of Amrita Devi and the 363 martyrs is a foundational story: it reminds them how to act. I understand the narrative well enough, but I clearly don't understand trees in the way the Bishnoi do. That's the understanding I need, how a person can value a tree's life more than their own, and I'll go wherever I'm taken to discover it. For now, I'm strapped in a car on an outing to who knows where, expectant and ripe for wonder.

On the rim of the city a road rises up a hillside. The hill is a sand dune. It blew into place as sand dunes do but then shrubs and trees grew roots to stop it moving further. We ascend this dune. Ram Niwas parks the car and gestures me to step out.

It's a sound I hear first, like a shallow stream rushing over pebbles, but that's not what it is. This is desert with no such streams. Around me bare ground is studded with stones. And a mass of rounded grey boulders ... that are moving.

Those grey boulders are the round bodies of a vast flock of birds, their long black necks dipping heads toward ground. White feathers shoot a plume from behind their red eyes. The sound I hear is a gurgling in their throats. They are hundreds of demoiselle cranes, feeding off scattered grain.

Ram Niwas signals me to stay and watch. I find more crowds of birds, all feasting, while some beat their wings to fly their silhouettes against the dawn sky. They bred in Mongolia and the Caucasus and then flew over the Himalayas to get here, a two-week journey at altitudes up to 20,000 feet, melanin painting their wingtips black to toughen them against fierce winds. They land here each December, glad of a milder winter, and stay into March.

Demoiselles are thirty inches tall and weigh just over six pounds, the smallest of cranes but still bigger than a Canada goose and heavier than a great blue heron. Cranes mate for life, and in their pairs they dance. The larger species such as sandhill cranes indulge in gymnastic leaps, but the demoiselles move as in a ballet. Their dance is an act of ecstatic mirroring.

Valmiki, the bard who wrote the sacred Indian epic the *Ramayana*, once saw a hunter kill a demoiselle crane. Its female partner danced a spiral of grief around her dead mate, her long neck straightening and twisting, a lament keening from her throat. Touched by the horror of what he had witnessed the poet told the tale in verse. The *Ramayana* is viewed as a text channelled from divine sources. In contrast, this verse tale of the cranes came not from the gods but from the poet's pained human response to the male crane's killing and then witnessing the female's grief.

Poetry's human origins were thus sparked by destruction in the natural world.

The sounds of gurgling cranes lead me around a temple's high earthen walls. This is the Bishnoi temple of Jajiwal Dhora, and after a further circuit of crane-watching I enter through its gates.

I thought to find Ram Niwas but all I see is a small shrine on an empty earthen floor. Inside the shrine, seen through open doors, is a portrait of Jambhoji. Bishnois say that name often, and with fondness. He was their founding guru, shown with hair and beard in long white tresses, wearing a saffron robe and a conical saffron cap. Early morning worshippers have already come to this temple shrine and gone away, leaving a fire burned to ashes on a tray outside.

I come upon Ram Niwas on the far side of the shrine, beside a teenage priest who smiles and ushers me through a gate. Inside an enclosure I am suddenly surrounded by infant reddish-brown gazelles. It's a species known as chinkara. Even with their large pointed ears these young ones are no higher than my knee and they push at me with their heads, grapple my sides with their front legs, pull threads from my jacket with their teeth.

These chinkara are orphans, and part of the temple's mission is to nurture them till they are old enough to re-enter the wild. The priest looks after a further pen containing young and wounded blackbuck, a desert antelope, and it is he in his saffron clothes and sandals who at dawn carries and spreads the grain for the demoiselle cranes.

The species' name, 'chinkara', denoting a sneeze, derives from this gazelle's alarm call; when startled they stamp their front feet and emit a sneeze-like cry. Bishnoi children are made sensitive to this chinkara sneeze, ready to run to the animal's rescue when they hear the sound.

We now head to meet some of those children. Ram Niwas drives to a small nearby town and turns through an archway into the courtyard of a school.

Ram Niwas is an entrepreneur after my own heart, in that his ventures don't make money. He is a social entrepreneur, out to do good. This school, the Saviour Children's Academy, is one of his biggest ventures. School fees are kept just high enough to pay the teachers' salaries: the whole point of the school is to give an English-language education to Bishnoi children that is affordable and not far from home.

A class of children, around twelve years old, are happy to talk to me in English. They sit in their dark green uniforms behind wooden desks, the girls with bright red ribbons at the ends of their pigtails.

I am a writer, I say. If you were writing a book what would you want it to say?

Chanchai, a girl in the middle of the classroom, puts up her hand. 'We must protect birds, animals and trees – do not cut the trees and kill the birds.'

At the very front, Santosh, her round face supremely confident and smiling widely, raises her hand. 'Trees give us oxygen and without oxygen we cannot live.' Santosh then questions me. 'What is happiness?'

I give her my answer and ask for hers.

'Taking care of the small things.'

What about ambition? What would she like to be when she grows up?

'A good citizen.'

What makes a good citizen?

Santosh is unfazed. 'Helping the development of my country India, and caring for others.'

At the front a slender boy raises his hand. Yuvraj is the one child with a *bindi* marked onto his brow, a thumbprint of ash from the fire of the morning's Bishnoi ritual. He's been thinking through this matter and has one thing to add: 'Remember the three hundred and sixty-three people who died at the nearby village of Khejarli to protect the trees.'

Why did they do that? I ask him. Weren't their lives as important as trees? Would he die for a tree?

Yes he would. 'Trees are for all,' he answers. 'I am for just one family.'

And he has more advice. 'You must visit Khejarli.'

On the road to Khejarli, Ram Niwas pulls into the side, opens his door, slides out, and makes sure I do the same without making a noise. 'Look!' an urgent whisper. 'Look!'

I look. A field of tall grasses.

And yes! Animals. A herd of what would be deer where I come from. They're tawny but with white bellies and rumps, and erect pointed ears like a giant jackrabbit's or hare's. There are twelve of them. These are females, not deer but ...

Ram Niwas is waving his hand, not there, look left, left.

And I see where he is pointing and draw breath.

Those females were blackbuck and this one is a male, his upper body black. White patches like goggles ring his eyes. His chest is broad and solid, while his horns, black and spiralling high as twin corkscrew shafts, pierce the sky three feet above his head. He looks as mythical as a unicorn. The female blackbucks stand in a group and he is separate but of course he's not, he is emitting a force field that contains the herd who graze placidly within its protection. His eyes are on us, probing for danger. Blackbuck and chinkara recognise Bishnois, their men in white clothing, as their friends. Ram Niwas passes muster.

Spring rutting season is about to start. No other adult males are allowed inside his acreage. These blackbuck are grazing now, but can reach speeds of sixty miles an hour. Marked as 'Near Threatened' on the United Nations Red List, an inventory of the conservation status of biological species, about forty thousand blackbuck live in India, mostly in Rajasthan. Herds are strongest in areas controlled by the Bishnoi.[2]

The male blackbuck is growing restless.

Time to leave them. They were a bonus. Ram Niwas has a treasured place to show me. It's close.

Local Bishnois run an animal rescue centre beside the road. That's handy, seeing as many animals come here when struck by traffic. Others are savaged by feral dogs. One baby chinkara is in its own pen, a dog bite gouged into its leg. Ram Niwas takes it into his hands, hoists it in the air and holds it nose to nose, presses it to his chest and against his heartbeat, as his eyes grow moist. Is he being sentimental? Does he really see this animal as being like his own injured child?

Yes, that's how he sees it.

A newly planted garden surrounds the animal sanctuary's walls, filled with 363 young trees, one for each of the Khejarli martyrs. The site of the massacre is further along the road. The highway has ripped away Khejarli's remoteness. Our car slots into the traffic of trucks that thunders through the town. Store owners slump on wooden chairs outside their shop doors; the town's string of low buildings are dirty and crumbling.

A mile further on is the site of the massacre, wrapped inside high walls of white stone. Each September many thousands pack the place, gathering for speeches, remembering the martyrs on the anniversary of their deaths, chanting the words of their Guru Jambhoji and singing devotional songs around sacred flames. They buy khejri seedlings from the forestry department's stands and take them to plant at their homes. Large enough for a fleet of buses, today the gravel car park is empty. Peacocks scuttle between the trees, surprised at human interruption.

The khejri trees near the opening are fairly young, with trunks you can wrap inside two hands. Khejris are evergreens, their leaves a dark blue-green, and what leaves they shed fall at the end of winter. It's now January, with just a thin scattering of leaves on the higher branches. I touch the trunk of one, feel its dryness, hug my arms around it, move on.

I'm looking for some large trees, ones that could be hugged by those martyrs, but the ones I find are not khejris but jaal, handsome trees that don't burn with the intense heat of the hardwood khejri. These are twenty-five feet tall, their broad bases ringed by concrete and their trunks so thick, like several trees twined into one, that several people would need to hold hands to hug. Their leaf-thick crowns cast shadows that touch an old temple, small and white and boxlike. Two battered panels sit on the floor of its whitewashed interior. They are graphic paintings of Amrita and her daughters' beheadings.

The chip-chip of stonemasons' axes directs us to a new temple. Built of pink and cream stone, its three domes let in light to illuminate the sandstone carvings on its walls. They reveal the narrative of the massacre. You see villagers at prayer around the fire in the morning ritual that started that tragic day. The men walk off to their day's work while the women and their young daughters stay behind and draw water from a well, kept company by a small gazelle. Their homes are small and round and roofed by thatch. The Maharajah's men arrive. Tragedy ensues.

The original memorial to the 363 martyrs is an austere thirty-foot high cenotaph, a solid block of sandstone topped like a battlement. Masons are working on a fresh memorial, carving the martyrs' names on a circle of giant slabs. Inside a pagoda at the centre of the circle stands a statue of Amrita Devi. Is it a statue? She moved, didn't she? And it's so: the statue is dressed in a cotton saree that stirs in the breeze.

The khejri trees here are newly planted saplings. Ram Niwas leads me between them. He has spotted someone, a slender, smiling man with close-cropped grey hair, in a singlet and *dhoti*, his red sandals on the floor, sitting cross-legged on a cot with a walking stick hanging from it. This is the priest of Khejarli. He explains that he has knee trouble. Me too, I say, but at least you can sit cross-legged.

'By the grace of Jambhoji,' and he raises his hands and spreads his fingers and looks up into the sky.

His gaze into the heavens gives him words to describe this sad site. 'This is the only place in Rajasthan, in India, in the whole world, that honours a community who gave their lives to save the environment,' he says. 'That is our message to the world.'

3

Bishnois versus Salman Khan

A FEW MILES ON FROM KHEJARLI, beside the highway, is a bare concrete platform raised above road level. You want the bathroom? It's at the back. Which means pick your way through the rubbish and go where you like. This is a roadside restaurant with a roof but no walls. This highway is at the fringe of the village of Kankani and we are hosted by the restaurant's owner Hiram Ram Bishnoi. He is also the village *serpench*, its elected chief official, greying hair beneath his white turban. He looks to the side as he speaks, recalling the events of 1998 when events here became world headline news. His village is where the most famous man in India came with night-vision goggles.[3] And came up against Hiram Ram's uncle and cousins.

This world-famous invader was the film star Salman Khan, a man regularly topping the Forbes Indian Celebrity List for fame and fortune, then in his early thirties. Filming for his latest all-star family drama began in Mumbai, but in October of that year the film's cast and crew moved up to Jodhpur. The city has world-class hotels, and a short drive away cameras can pan across the compelling desert scenery of Rajasthan. Designed to be that year's blockbuster, *Hum Saath Saath Hain* ('We Stand United') was set for some weeks of location shooting. Even among an all-star Bollywood cast, Salman Khan was stellar; he would appear in a record ten of the top-grossing films that year. In Western terms, think Tom Cruise or Brad Pitt.

Pump out star quality on the set all day, and at night you're still burning. Who needs bed? As night cloaked the desert, Salman Khan shot out on an off-road trip with a jeep and a driver. Allegedly, when he returned it was with the body of a chinkara. They're small, these tiny gazelles, and fast, and so rare they have been given special legal protection. A story told of a night-time chinkara feast back at the actor's hotel. If so, defending counsel would say at a future trial, bring us the knife with which you say Salman Khan fleeced the chinkara.[4] And where is the driver? Journalists tracked him down. Yes, the driver told them, he saw Khan shoot the animal. So why didn't he show up in court? He had been threatened, he said.[5]

On 2 October 1998 other cast members joined Khan in his jeep.[6] As per claims, they were after blackbuck. Only an Indian cheetah, now extinct, ran faster and though cheetahs could leap far they couldn't leap as high as blackbuck do. Blackbucks are endangered and officially protected, which is why the film party came out in the secrecy of night. With their bursts of speed and crazy leaps, blackbucks are a challenge to shoot. And the males with those long twin horns that corkscrew high above their heads, that's the sort of beast a hunter mounts for display on his wall.

Twenty minutes out of Jodhpur, by the village of Kankani, the party turned off-road, headlights sweeping desert. They swerved round the trees and churned up sand. Ahead of them creatures were running fast. Bang. Bang. The animals fell. The jeep, allegedly filled with the actors, raced toward the kill, stopped, and the actors got out.

Hiram Ram looked away from his restaurant, toward his village of Kankani, and spoke of what happened then. In the nearby house his nephew's family was yet to settle. His nephew had sold a buffalo and its new owners had just left. Up on the roof, his daughter-in-law saw the lights of a jeep bouncing through the night, its engine roaring. She let out a shout.

Her husband, Choga Ram, called to his brother Poonamchand and both men jumped on a scooter and raced to the scene. They saw a jeep, the people beside it, and in the light from their scooter they recognised the actor Salman Khan. Who wouldn't?

The actors jumped into their jeep and doors slammed shut even while the wheels span and the vehicle drove away. The scooter's lights fell on the scene the actors had left behind, one to make a Bishnoi weep: the bodies of two slain blackbuck.

The men revved up their scooter. The actors did not know about a check post on the road ahead. The jeep would turn to avoid it and come back their way. The two brothers and their father were waiting, one with a large stick. The jeep came, the stick smashed into its side, but the jeep swerved and drove away.

Poonamchand noted down the number of their licence plate. A villager recognised the fleeing jeep as belonging to a tour operator that he knew. A crowd of Bishnois tracked the jeep back to Salman Khan's hotel. In the morning they laid siege to the place, shouting for justice. The police and the government had to respond and start an investigation.

The crime scene was intact, the corpses of the blackbuck stretched where they landed on the blood-soaked dirt, a group of Bishnoi men standing vigil. This is what Bishnois do: protect the evidence till the authorities come. The carcases were carried away for postmortem examination.

Who better to do the work than Rajasthan's chief veterinary officer? Well, just about anybody. The causes of the blackbucks' death were two-fold, the officer declared. One blackbuck had fallen in a hole. The other had been killed by a dog.[7]

You call in the law to resolve this illegal killing of endangered animals, and this is what happens. What else can you do?

Shine a light on the state veterinarian, for a start. Which is what the Bishnoi did. Criminal proceedings were set in motion against the veterinarian and were only dropped when he died.[8] Meantime, a new postmortem identified bullet wounds.[9] The blackbuck had died from gunfire. But were these animals dug up from their grave verifiably blackbuck?

The blackbuck's special legal protection almost aggrieves the Bishnoi. 'Being nature lovers to the core,' notes the journalist Gangadharan Menon, 'they bemoan the fact that, under the Indian Wildlife Act, animals are accorded various levels of importance. But to a Bishnoi, killing a monitor lizard is as hideous a crime as killing a tiger. To them, every life has value.'[10]

However, since the ways of the modern world are stacked up against the needs of wildlife, Bishnois will use whatever scrap of legal support is available to them. And forest officers help. Alert to the need for evidence strong enough to withstand the keen scrutiny of a court hearing, the young officer who had exhumed the blackbuck corpses called in DNA experts. DNA scraped from the carcases was compared with blood samples from blackbucks at Hyderabad Zoo. For the first time the same science used to identify human remains was used to identify animals. These exhumed bodies were indeed blackbuck. And so, with the special protection given to these animals under law, their killing was indeed a crime.[11]

In a legal battle, take on the Indian film industry and its leading star and you don't want to be a lone villager. You'll be squashed. But Poonamchand, who was the Bishnois' principle witness at the scene, had his religion to empower him. Beyond that, he had the Bishnoi community. In the wake of Khan's blackbuck killing, the recently formed Bishnoi Tiger Force, a vigilante group, had a huge boost in membership and a powerful sense of purpose. They deputed guards to protect their witness. And they formed mock courts at which Poonamchand could practise giving his deposition before a magistrate.

Lalit Bora was the investigating officer working for the police. 'We had circumstantial evidence and seizures of articles to prove that poaching was done,' he said. But he agreed that it was the eyewitnesses and their testimony that swayed the case.[12]

One such eyewitness was the driver of the hunting party's jeep, Harish Dulani. In the lower court trial he testified that it was Salman Khan who had done the shooting.

The legal process ground on. And on. And the Bishnois stayed the course, a Bishnoi lawyer assisting the state attorneys.

One decade passed. Salman Khan's legal team are highly invested in delaying any trial.

A second decade passed. Khan's legal team are as good as it gets. But the Bishnoi have become an implacable force.[13] 'Khan waged an all-out defense,' noted *The Los Angeles Times*, 'with film industry luminaries and legions of fans demanding his exoneration and lawyers stalling the proceedings so many times that the lead witness, a Bishnoi villager [Poonamchand], had to appear in court 68 times.'[14]

In 2018, twenty years after the alleged crime, a police force of two hundred were deployed outside the courthouse to control any possible disturbance. Flanked by his own security guard, Salman Khan arrived in black shirt and jeans and wearing dark glasses. In reading out the verdict, the chief magistrate termed the actor 'a habitual offender'.[15] The verdict? Five years in jail.

Firecrackers jumped and exploded across the street outside the court. Bishnois were celebrating. How did Poonamchand feel, all these decades after racing his scooter to the scene of the blackbuck slaughter? 'Fulfilled!'

Was Rampal Bishnoi, state president of the Bishnoi Tiger Force, happy? 'Though the sentence should have been bigger,' he told reporters, 'as he killed two blackbucks, we are satisfied that the court found him guilty and handed him a fitting sentence.'[16] Khan's fellow actors were acquitted. Not good enough, declared Rampal Bishnoi. The Tiger Force would find ways to appeal their acquittals.

In the years between the blackbuck killings and Khan's guilty verdict, the Tiger Force had teamed up with law enforcers. 'Bishnois have over the years become our partners,' said a senior police officer in Jodhpur, 'especially the leaders and volunteers of the Bishnoi Tiger Force. They maintain information networks to bust poaching all over western Rajasthan. At times, they accompany us to remotest desert areas owing to their familiarity of the terrain.'

On these far-flung raids do the police have to keep the Bishnoi men in check? Never. In all the pursuits of poachers the policeman can't recall a single incident where Bishnois used a weapon or turned violent.[17] That's despite more than two dozen members of the Tiger Force being killed in action during these years.

'We have registered more than 400 cases so far,' the Tiger Force president reflected from the courtroom steps. 'And we make sure that the witnesses in our cases stand their ground in courts. We hold mock courts to train them on how to depose before magistrates and motivate them to remain firm during the trial of the cases.'[18]

Khan, of course, had his own brilliant legal team on the case. He spent a few days behind bars then was released on bail, pending his appeal.

Over lunch at the roadside restaurant men reconstruct the remains of the story.

What was the cause for Khan's legal appeal? At that first trial in the lower court, Khan's legal team had turned down the right to produce evidence for the defence.[19] The driver who testified against Khan subsequently vanished for a while.

When he reappeared, he had changed his story.[20] With the case now in the Higher Court, Khan's lawyers claimed the lower court had refused them the opportunity to cross-examine witnesses. The judge declared a mistrial, and the case moved on to the Supreme Court.

Khan was banned from overseas travel.[21] Then the Covid pandemic gave cause to delay any new court appearances.[22] As of October 2024 there had been fifteen separate court actions in the ongoing trial.

Back in 1999, the Tiger Force's new members were young, including the teenage Ram Niwas. When the film from Khan's Rajasthan shoot, *Hum Saath Saath Hain*, was set for its glitzy Jodhpur premiere, he joined the Tiger Force in a street demonstration that kept the cinema closed for the night.

Of course, the men of the Bishnoi Tiger Force held an alternative view of Salman Khan to many Indians. An Indian journalist tells how, for the actor's mostly male followers, 'Khan's bad-boy image has sustained him from the beginning of his career. The frequent reports of drunken misbehaviour in public, indiscipline at work and girlfriend abuse, along with the hit-and-run and poaching cases that finally landed him in court, have contributed greatly to fan enthusiasm.'[23]

Twenty-two years later, Jodhpur invited Khan to start the Jodhpur Marathon. Fifty members of the Tiger Force made sure he was turned away. 'How can someone start a marathon here when he killed blackbuck,' Ram Niwas says, 'the state animal of Rajasthan?'

Two other Bishnois have dominated recent Indian newspaper headlines.

One is Ravi Bishnoi, who you'll find in the sports pages. Bishnois are not known for sporting achievements, and so the teenage Ravi had to carry rocks from barren ground and haul cement to help build his training base. With friends he sowed the land with grass, brought in special red mud for the wicket, levelled the ground, and Jodhpur's Spartans Cricket Academy was formed. His coaches gave him a bike so he could cycle the fifteen miles to and from the ground at the beginning and end of each working day.

Better to focus on your exams, instructed his father, a school headmaster. More exciting to play cricket, said his mother, who was passionate about the sport. The boy persisted and built expertise as a spin bowler. No cricketer from Rajasthan had played for India since independence. Now they have. In December 2023 Ravi Bishnoi became ranked the world number one bowler in short overs cricket.

'Look!' temple authorities told me, pointing to a photo of Ravi on stage in a temple hall. He was there to tell groups of schoolchildren about all they can achieve if they follow Bishnoi values.

These children won't be taught about Lawrence Bishnoi. Turn to the newspaper's front pages for stark headlines about him. 'Every society has its renegades,' Bishnois told me.

Lawrence Bishnoi is a bandit and a gang leader from the Punjab. His 'Bishnoi Gang' began in a trade that is the dark side of several Bishnoi communities: opium smuggling. They expanded into extortion and killings. Currently confined to a Delhi prison cell, Lawrence Bishnoi still wields influence over his gang members.

Are blackbucks the incarnation of Guru Jambhoji? Every Bishnoi I asked thought this was a crazy notion, all creatures being equally sacred, but multiple printed sources and also Lawrence Bishnoi hold this equivalence of guru and antelope to be indeed true. In 2022, from his prison cell, he announced that unless Salman Khan and his father attend the Bishnois' main temple and offer a public apology for slaying the blackbuck, he would have them both killed.[24]

Salman Khan normally meets crowds of his fans for the festival of Eid, which closes the Muslim fasting period of Ramadan. That year he locked himself away. Fifteen security cameras swept around his apartment building and ten special forces officers were assigned to his protection. In the summer Mumbai police authorised Khan to carry a personal firearm, and the actor went on to add armour and bulletproof glass to his Toyota Landcruiser.[25] Feeling the need of still more security, in 2023 he imported a bulletproof armoured Nissan Patrol from Dubai.[26]

In April 2024, at 5am on a Sunday morning, he was asleep inside his Mumbai apartment. Two young men on a motor-bike fired shots into his front door, and then raced off firing shots into the air. Both were later apprehended. One soon died under police interrogation, allegedly by suicide.[27]

Worried for Salman Khan's life, his ex-girlfriend pleaded with the Bishnois to forgive him.

'If he himself comes to the temple and seeks forgiveness,' said Devendra Budiya, president of the All India Bishnoi Society, 'our community could think about forgiving him, because one of our twenty-nine rules is forgiveness. Salman should further take an oath that he will never make such a mistake again and will work to protect wildlife and the environment.'[28]

Was Ram Niwas secretly pleased at these death threats to Salman Khan? The suggestion shocks him. 'We are non-violent people. What is the difference between us and Salman Khan if we kill him? We want the process of the law to take place. When he came up to Jodhpur for the trial we could have caused trouble, but we didn't.'

Across the highway from the restaurant, deeper into the village, workers are finishing a large stone platform. This is at the site where Khan allegedly shot the blackbuck. On top of the platform will stand a life-sized blackbuck statue, its horns composed of actual blackbuck horn taken from animals found dead in the forest. The young Bishnois of Kankani raised funds to pay for the 800 kg statue. On the surrounding land they are planting a thousand trees and hope to build a blackbuck rescue centre. The killing happened before they were born.

'We want to send a message to people,' said Prem Saran, one of the project's young organisers, 'to protect flora and fauna like our community does, so that a repeat of the 1998 incident does not happen. The site where the memorial is being made is the same as where the blackbucks were buried. These animals are like our family and we can sacrifice our lives to protect them.'

---

* In October 2024 the Lawrence Bishnoi gang – reported to be 700 strong – became the centre of a major international dispute, when they were named by police as working with agents of the Indian government to assassinate a Sikh separatist living in Canada.

4

The Men Who Gave Their Lives for a Gazelle

SOMEHOW RAM NIWAS OPERATES WITHOUT MONEY. On the highway out of Jodhpur he talks to the tollbooth operators until they let him drive on without paying.

We're heading about ninety miles west. Where to? A 'mela' is all I know, some religious gathering. We swing off the highway and bomb along narrow country lanes lined with hedges. The Bishnoi commandment not to kill wildlife demands hyper-alertness. A lark drops from the hedge to land on the road in front of us. A creature charges across the road, slung low like a rat, bushy tailed like a squirrel, striped like a chipmunk. A tawny cat slinks out from a hedge and freezes in horror. We swerve and screech to a halt each time, Ram Niwas slamming on the brakes for the tyres to skid to a stop as the car fills with the stench of burned rubber. The creatures survive, we open the car windows to clear the rubber-infused air, and race on.

Ram Niwas keeps speaking to his phone. I hear my name, my nationality and the word *kitab*, that I know from my minimal Arabic means 'book' and now transfer across to my small store of Hindi. Ram Niwas finishes one conversation and starts another, explaining my existence, announcing my presence. And then we arrive at the *mela*. Minibuses and cars are parked on a patch of roadside dust beside a high pink wall, whose gates are open, and inside is a large tent.

At the front of the tent an orange banner features a young man in his twenties. Dark eyebrows curve in across his brow to give him a serious expression and his upper lip has the dusting of young moustache. He's dressed in a white shirt with an open collar. The script around him is in Hindi and a date is in the top right corner: 29.1.14. That was six years ago yesterday. This is the anniversary of his funeral. Inside the tent large groups of people are sitting on the floor and others on a stage and an amplified man's voice is speaking. Our real host, it seems, is this young man on the banner.

I piece together the story from a newspaper article I have read about a young man who gave his life to protect a chinkara. His photo is also on a larger banner stretched behind the dais, alongside Guru Jambhoji with his orange robes and flow of white beard, who is in the banner's top right corner. I'm settled on the dais.

'Father,' Ram Niwas says, and nods to a man on my right. This man is elderly, his grey moustache a smart handlebar. He wears a beige golfing cap rather than a turban, and a dark grey striped jacket. We mime a conversation with our hands and with our eyes – he pointing upward to his son in heaven, me patting my hand against my heart, looking up toward the spirit of his son and then bowing my head.

The young man on the banner is Shaitanaram Singh Bishnoi – Shaitan, for short – from the nearby village of Namu. His family owns twenty acres of land which they lease out for others to grow crops. Home is a six-roomed house, with bare walls and sparse furniture and no indoor toilet, as is the norm in a Bishnoi household, and it shelters a growing family. Until recently, child marriage was common among the Bishnoi. At the age of two Shaitan was married to two-year-old Pushpa. In 2007, when they were both eighteen, she moved in with him. By January 2014 they had two children, their daughter Jyoti and their baby son Pyush.

The chinkara gazelles, with their vulnerability and their beauty, are especially dear to Bishnois. Each morning they spread grain for the animals. Usually so wary of humans, the tiny gazelles flocked to this village of Namu like an extended family. Shaitan was a member of the Bishnoi Tiger Force. Back in 2012 he had given chase to a couple of chinkara poachers but there was no direct confrontation as they managed to escape on their motorbikes.

Four years later, and 28 January was the first new moon of 2016. Shaitan, his brother, and two labourers who worked for the family were in the city of Bikaner on business but caught the evening train home. Pushpa took her husband's phone call – he would be home at eleven. Could she have their dinner ready?

When they arrived, Pushpa fed the men and went to bed. Shaitan and his brother Manigal were too excited to sleep.

From her bed, Pushpa listened to the burble of the men's voices around the kitchen table. And then from outside she heard the shrill sneeze alarm call of the chinkara.

Pushpa went on alert. Their village was remote, and silent at night, yet now she heard the roar of a motorbike's engine. She rose from the bed and hurried to her husband. He mustn't go out, she told him. It's not safe. But the two brothers and the labourers were already running for their Bolero.

It became a chase, the SUV against two motorbikes, ridden by men who had to be poachers. At the wheel of the Bolero, Shaitan powered up his headlights and followed the bounce of the bikes' lights, along a dirt track at first, and then the poachers veered from the road and charged across rough ground. Soon both the SUV and the motorbike were stuck. Shaitan revved the engine but the wheels of the Bolero simply dug deeper into sand. The man on the bike was revving its engine too, while a second man had climbed off the bike in order to push it from behind.

'He's got a gun,' shouted Manigal, Shaitan's brother. He could see a shotgun in one of the poacher's hands, while the brothers were unarmed. 'Don't go, Shaitan.'

But Shaitan didn't listen. He jumped out of the SUV and charged. You can only grab one man at a time so Shaitan leapt for the rider. His brother and the two labourers were running to join him. He had the poacher in his grip.

To free his friend, the other poacher fired his double-barrelled twelve-bore shotgun. The shot blew through

Shaitan's head. Pushpa had run up to the roof of the house. She heard the blast of the gun. Then came Manigal's cry. 'They killed him!'

The following morning, at the spot where Shaitan fell, two thousand Bishnois gathered to grieve and remember him. A memorial topped by graceful sandstone arches was built on the hilltop nearby, visible from his home. People came from hundreds of miles around to pay their respects.

In a film made about the young man's martyrdom, Shaitan's father Arjunram, the man I met on the memorial ceremony dais, weeps when he speaks of his son. 'We are proud that he sacrificed himself for his beliefs. There is no escape from sorrow but he died doing his duty. We were family, we were happy, but now no more. What can be done about it? It hurts. Sometimes I wonder when Shaitan will return, then I remember he has passed on. But my heart wishes he would return. We are helpless.'

Pushpa adopts orphaned chinkara into her family. In the film one wobbles through the courtyard and suckles from the teat of a bottle. She will remain a widow, she has decided. What about her little son Pyush? Were he to face the same situation as his father, seeing a need to run unarmed to tackle an armed poacher, should he go?

Of course. 'Animals need to be protected first,' Pushpa explains. 'Humans can defend themselves.'[29]

The orange canopied roof for this *mela* is held up by thin wooden poles, panelled with a sunlike motif. Looking out from the dais, women sit on green carpet to the left. Pushpa is among the women, her red dress patterned with gold and a thick diagonal stripe of flowered blue. Her face is veiled. Her daughter Jyoti is almost a teenager now, in a bright yellow dress with short sleeves. Her son Pyush is still young enough to be on the women's side, and dressed in a brushed cotton shirt of red tartan. Both children wear gold lockets high on their throats.

To the right are the men, all in white, many with white turbans. Far to my right a young priest in his orange robes tends an open fire. Men come forward to drink ghee warmed by the fire and drop banknotes onto a tray, and when the men are done the women follow. Speaker after speaker comes to the white podium. In the far distance I look out on the sunlight and the domed temple. A bony white cow steps inside the tent and young men usher it away.

All stand for the entry of an eminent, rounded priest in orange turban and robes, who is the head of Jambaji temple, which we can see through the opening of the tent. This is one of two principal Bishnoi temples, and as its high priest he is the head of the Bishnoi priesthood. Later, when a slender man with full white hair and trim moustache and a Nehru suit enters the congregation, everybody else stands up, but this priest remains sitting.

Ram Niwas takes the microphone. The atmosphere becomes charged. The crowd leans forward, compelled. Gaps in Ram Niwas's speech meet with voiced rushes of approval. His speech is fiery.

I understand nothing but then I hear my name, and the words Bishnoi and London and '*kitab*'. He has been plotting this all along, I later learn. The congregation have been donating money for a statue of Shaitan to be erected. 'I have no money to give,' Ram Niwas is telling the audience. 'Instead I have brought you a writer who will write a book in English and tell your story to the world.'

Then the man in the Nehru suit, cream jacket above white trousers, takes his turn. This is Pabbaram Bishnoi, the local Member of the State Legislative Assembly. He switches from Hindi to English and addresses me directly. How unique and important the Bishnoi are in the world, he explains. No other group will give its life to protect animals. He turns back to the audience, back to Hindi, before returning to English and to me. 'Take your book seriously,' he exhorts me, and with his words the book seems to have been commissioned. I must visit the main sites of prayer and gatherings for the Bishnoi people, he urges, naming each one. I must tell the world about these places and the Bishnoi and their beliefs.

Before entering politics, Pabbaram was a headmaster and now he gives me a headmasterly stare. The high priest turns his face to me, impassive, waiting. The congregation remains stilled.

Placing my hand on my chest above my heart, I bow my head.

Yes, my gesture says.

Pabbaram smiles and nods. The high priest nods without smiling. The congregation relaxes into a murmur of conversation.

Their job is done.

The ceremony rounds off with awards for environmental service. I help hand out the certificates and plaques and am awarded one of each myself, for a book I have committed to write.

The moment I am released from the podium a young girl runs up to speak to me. This is Jyoti, Shaitan and Pushpa's daughter, bright and confident and keen to practise her English. With her are Pushpa, the widow, hidden behind her veil; the young son Pyush, with his bright smile; and Shaitan's father Arjunram with a white scarf draped across his shoulder.

They are pleased I am to tell their story.

Out beyond the tent is the desert, and a temple in its distance has been framed by the tent's opening, like the cover of a guidebook. Ram Niwas now drives us the short distance to the temple, along the four-hundred-yards-wide edge of a reservoir. Its water is sixty feet deep and stretches two thousand yards in length, a true desert phenomenon.

The origin of this reservoir is a venerated tale from Bishnoi history. Back in the fifteenth century the ruler of the state of Jaisalmer, Rawal Jait Singh, had built a new water tank. When he invited Jambhoji to give this tank his inaugural blessing, Jambhoji agreed. In return the Rawal asked what he might do for Jambhoji.

Many animals had been brought to the ceremony, to be slaughtered and fed to the congregation. Let them be spared, Jambhoji asked. And in future no animal should be killed when it is pregnant. One tribal group in the state, the Bawariyas, took their name from the *bawar* noose with which they caught wild animals. Their hunts should be banned, said the guru. And all stolen cattle should be returned to their owners, even if that meant herding them back across state lines.

The Rawal agreed to all four requests. In addition, he laid a purse filled with money at Jambhoji's feet. The guru refused the gift, but the Rawal explained it had already been withdrawn from his treasury and so could not be returned. In that case, Jambhoji decided, there had once been a water tank in the town of Jambha that had been abandoned and dried up; let the money be used to build a new one.

When the project went ahead, one thousand seven hundred Bishnois took part in the digging. That was the reservoir we were now approaching.

I take off my shoes and socks in the way Ram Niwas demonstrates and follow him down stone steps to the reservoir's edge. I wash my hands and feet and cup water up to stream across my face, and its taste on my lips teaches me that this inland water is salty. Above us, twenty-six demoiselle cranes stretch forward their black necks and trail their long legs as they fly in formation across the blue. We are now cleansed and ready to enter the temple.

The temple on the banks of this reservoir is known as Jambaji. Barefoot, we cross rough ground to the smooth marble of the temple's courtyard. A man in dark dress comes from the temple toward us. He is 'the chief' of the community and had left the memorial service just before us. This temple replaces an old one, he tells me, and is receiving its finishing touches under his watch.

'You know Ganga?' he asks, speaking of the Ganges. It's a simple question but conjures images from my visits to that

river: the crowds bathing on the ghats at Varanasi; a woman throwing cremated ashes from a swing bridge at Rishikesh. 'Well, for us this water is as sacred as Ganga.'

The chief heads away and we walk on across the courtyard to the temple. Its dome caps empty space but at its heart stands a white stone shrine with six-foot-high wooden doors across an archway that Ram Niwas pulls open. He reveals a chamber, currently empty save for a large gold-framed painting of the head of Guru Jambhoji, his hands clasped in front of his thick white beard. Saffron cloth is draped wide from the sides of the frame, which stands on a low table among garlands of marigolds.

Ram Niwas clasps his hands and bows in reverence, and has me do the same, and we walk the shrine's perimeter before coming back to its opening. The small fire that fuelled that morning's ceremony has gone out, but Ram Niwas kneels. He daubs its ash between my brows and then marks this ashen *bindi* on his own brow. With my hands clasped in front of my heart I *namaste* to the portrait of Jambhoji. It is as though, having engaged me to write the book of the Bishnoi, he is concluding the business by presenting me to his guru.

Ram Niwas closes the doors of the shrine and we head to the monastery in search of food.

There is no formal training college for becoming a Bishnoi priest: instead, boys and men choose a priest as their guru and enter a period of discipleship. This can last fifteen to twenty years. The novices learn how to run the services and how to support their religion, they study the scriptures, and when the priest sees it right to ordain them, the disciple will put on his saffron robes and come here, to the monastery at Jambha. He calls in all the existing priests, feeds them, and offers himself as part of their community.

We sit among a crowd of young orange-clad priests and eat the lentils that are spooned onto our tin platters. It's my first food of the day.

As we start our return drive the sky is dimming to dusk. Where hundreds of doves sit wing to wing on roadside strands of telegraph wire, we turn right, up a road that leads to the top of a hill. A simple building of two rooms and a courtyard is up here and I presume Ram Niwas has some business inside, but he simply stands and waits for me to climb out.

I find myself among young chinkara, seven of them with their tan bodies and white underbellies. Their heads are the height of my chest, and when I hold out the flat palm of my hand they approach warily, shivers of fear passing up from their necks to their ears, bowing their heads to show me their ridged horns before dancing backward on spindly legs.

During his fifteenth-century wanderings, Guru Jambhoji once camped here to preach nature conservation. Nearby is the village of Lohawat: a square hilltop building is a community centre, on its flank is a small temple, and across the road from the bottom of the hill is a small shrine. The surrounding acreage of countryside is Rajasthan's first community reserve, born of similar events to those that ended Shaitan's life.

We walk to the base of the hill, take off our shoes and pay homage to the bust of a man set atop a pink pedestal. The Hindi inscription names him as Birbal Bishnoi, born 15 January 1940 and died 17 December 1977. Like Shaitan, he was a local farmer, at home eating his dinner when he heard gunshots. He left his dinner and rushed outside.

In line with his beliefs, Birbal regarded the wild chinkara as being as vulnerable as little children, and in his care. They were under attack. Birbal heard men running. He shouted and gave chase till he was able to see two men. He ran faster, the gap closed, and he grabbed one of the poachers.

The other fired. Birbal was hit, he was dying, but he held on. With his remaining life force he clung on to the poacher till other villagers arrived and were able to arrest the man. Birbal died.

On the statue his hair is painted jet black, as are his eyebrows and handlebar moustache. He is looking out toward the dunes and the grazing animals.

Back in 1730, the three hundred and sixty-three Bishnois who were massacred to save the trees at Khejarli came from eighty-three different villages. Lohawat was not one of those. Now, though, the village had its own martyr. Birbal's widow was presented with a medal from the President of India. A fund provided education for their children and a dowry for their daughter.

Ram Niwas had introduced me to the story of a recent martyr, and to the statue of another who had been killed before he was born. My research would teach me about many more Bishnois risking lives to save wildlife. One trove of stories happened in the area around Lohawat.[30] In 1979, two years after Birbal's death, there had been twenty-five actions against poachers. In one instance a man was protecting a hare, and in the others the villagers were defending chinkaras. In the first entry, from 19 January, five poachers had shot chinkara and one was caught. He 'was beaten until he confessed and vowed not to indulge in such crimes ever again in his life'. The dead chinkara was given a ritual burial, wrapped in linen. The poacher's fine paid for a memorial platform in the chinkara's honour.

Another incident in October 1979 saw a Jodhpur-bound bus driver run over a chinkara and load the dead animal into his bus to take home, where he planned to butcher it for food. A Bishnoi man on board objected so forcefully he was ejected from the bus. Undaunted, he hitched a sequence of lifts, overtook the bus, 'gathered fellow Bishnois and swooped on the driver at Jodhpur bus station. The driver was made to apologize and the body was given a burial.'[31]

In one of those twenty-five cases from 1979, the Bishnoi who pursued the poachers was shot and killed. Yet another in the annual count of Bishnoi martyrs.

Here's a more recent tale of a Bishnoi teenager in a village not far from Lohawat. It took place in May 2020. With schools shut due to the Covid pandemic, seventeen-year-old Mukesh Bishnoi studied his maths and social studies by day. At night he joined the community vigil. Lockdown had increased the rate of poaching so a fifteen-strong group had upped their 8pm till 3am patrols from twice a week to every night.

It was 8.30 in the evening. Mukesh and his friend were in the jeep on their way to their patrol area when they heard a gunshot. They raced toward it. Four men were distant specks at first, on a sand dune. At the sound of the jeep they started to hurry. Two carried guns, and the other two were carrying the body of a chinkara they had killed. The jeep wove round shrubs, coursed over a sand dune, but the wheels bit into deep sand and got stuck.

Mukesh quit the vehicle and charged across the desert on foot. A poacher raised his gun toward him. Mukesh hurled himself forward. As he caught hold of the poacher and grabbed hold of his gun, the two men with the chinkara ran on but that still left two against one. In the ensuing tussle, Mukesh was knocked off his feet and tumbled down the dune. He kept his grip on the gun, though. The poachers knew it had shot its bullets and was now not loaded and so not worth the fight. They ran.

The two friends sent a message to their WhatsApp group: 'A chinkara has been hunted. Come fast.' The first friends were there in ten minutes, and inside fifteen a hundred villagers had answered the call.

Shoot a chinkara, shift its weight between you as you carry it over deep sand, and it bleeds. The Bishnoi villagers started their search at the scene of the killing, and traced a blood trail for half a mile, a mile, the blood still dripping five miles away. The trail led to the door of a house in the village of Chamu. Officers from the forestry department were called and raided the house. Within, they found a weapon, but the poachers had fled. Nevertheless the officers knew who to look for.

Hadn't Mukesh been worried, tackling armed men?

His mother, he admitted, was petrified. Mukesh was her youngest child. But no, he hadn't been scared.

And he gave voice to what Shaitan might have said, had he not been killed.

'Saving chinkaras is my religion.'[32]

5

The Birth of Guru Jambhoji

WRITE ABOUT FOUNDERS OF RELIGIONS and you're wrestling with clouds. Try to pin them to a story that makes human sense and they don't play along. For them, taking human form was compromise enough. They need us to see beyond that form.

'My body is born because of my parents but I am beyond body and blood,' Jambhoji would say. 'I am all-pervading. There is nothing that I do not know and there is no one who does not know me. In other words, I am in everything and everything is in me.'

Fair enough. But we've got to start somewhere. Let's start with the parents, in the year before their son was born.

They live in the village of Pipasar, truly rural, thirty miles north of the nearest town of Naur and further still from the city of Bikaner. This is desert land that is easily exhausted, made of sand, scrub and winds. Yet visit Pipasar and you'll learn why Jambhoji grew up to be so fond of dunes.

His family house still stands, white rooms ranged around a courtyard. An old shrine to Jambhoji displays his sandals, and portraits depict him when young, his long beard black. Climb the stone stairs to the building's roof, gaze out on a panorama of crisp skies and low rounded hills, paint it and you have a landscape like the backdrops of Renaissance Madonnas.

These hills don't blaze green, of course, they're sand dunes, but shrubs grow into their sides and trees silhouette their rims. Winds blew the dunes into shape, and on their lee side the dunes protect farmland so topsoil doesn't blow away.

The Madonna of this story is Hansa. She has a fine home, she and her husband Lohat share devotion to the supreme god Vishnu, and they farm a good deal of the surrounding land. Yet Hansa doesn't feel blessed. For twenty years she has been trying for a child. Now she fears she is growing too old.

The strain is telling on Lohat. He goes out for an early morning walk to clear his head. Ahead on the path he spots a neighbour carrying a sack of millet seed. His heart lifts a little. It's good to find company, to share a few words.

But the neighbour pauses. Under the weight of the sack his head was bent toward the ground, but now he has spotted Lohat. He turns around, his legs kicking up speed as he carries the sack back home.

Why should his neighbour turn away from him like this, and flee? Lohat is puzzled, but only for a moment.

The answer comes, and it is the sort that blurs your vision for a while, stops you seeing. It's what happens when your secret shame goes public. A belief holds strong in the village: pass someone childless on your way to sow seeds, and those seeds will not germinate. A man carrying seed to his field has just run from Lohat in fear.

Lohat is a leading landowner, an eminent man in the village, yet this is how he is seen, he now knows. Simple villagers, with children of their own, see him as a barren man. As cursed.

The fact tips Lohat into despair.

When you feel such shame as he feels now you long to hide. Lohat veers off the track and takes shelter in a group of trees. What good was he? What use was all his devotion? 'I do all the good I know how to do,' he cries out to Vishnu. 'I don't take another wife who might give me a child. So why do you punish me like this?'

He drops to his knees and then to the ground, unconscious.

Who knows how long he is gone; he is in some place scraped clean of time. Now his eyes open and he sees blue sky, the boughs of trees, and the face of a sadhu, a wandering holy man, who is looking down at him.

'What is wrong?' the sadhu asks, with a voice so warm that Lohat finds the words to answer. He speaks of Hansa and her twenty years of yearning, that they both long for a child, that none has come, that she is getting too old, that villagers carrying seed view him as something barren, that all a man can do is stay true to his god but he must truly be bad because his wish for a child is simple but Vishnu will not grant it.

'Do not worry,' the sadhu says. 'Go home. Be with Hansa. You will have a son. And he will be the incarnation of Vishnu.'

Lohat hears the words, but how can they make sense?

He gets to his feet, set to challenge the sadhu, demand how the man can know such things. But the sadhu is gone. Lohat can't see him between the trees and when he is back on the track, looking left and right, the way is empty.

He hurries home. For twenty years he and Hansa have been trying for a child. Can it hurt them to try again? Lohat infuses her with his hope. Hansa takes comfort from her husband's tale of the sadhu and his words. They take to their bed.

From being an anxious woman, Hansa is filled with calm. Her stomach swells. They tell no one but as the months pass her pregnancy becomes obvious. Whatever the sadhu said to her husband, she doesn't feel the need to give birth to an incarnation of Vishnu. She wants only a son. But the couple are devotees of Vishnu and are cattle herders. Krishna the blue-faced god, ninth incarnation of Vishnu, was known as a herder of cattle and to be born on the same day as this god would be something special. That birthday falls on 8 August, a time of harvest. Hansa still has to work the fields that day. But her waters are breaking. Sooner than struggle home she lies down in a hut near the fields.

On 8 August 1451, she gives birth to her son.

They name the boy Jambho. Is this baby an incarnation of Vishnu? His aunt, Lohat's sister Tantu, is sure of it. Just look at the baby's face: it's utterly radiant.

Far away in a cave on the flank of a mountain, Yogi Rajendranatha, a famous yogi, felt the pangs of Hansa's labour and then the sudden freedom of a great being released to breathe the air of planet Earth. 'The Lord has taken fresh birth,' he told his devotees, and they all sang out in praise.

But baby Jambho won't breastfeed. He will not lie on his back. Even when asleep his eyes stay open, as though watching you. He shows almost no interest in food. And he is so silent. Is he perhaps both deaf and incapable of speech? When words do emerge, there's no making sense of them. Is he mumbling to himself maybe, or talking to some invisible companion?

'Gahla,' the villagers mutter to themselves, 'soft in the head'.

Hansa shares their fears. The boy is set for his seventh birthday. How much longer can they wait for him to act sensibly?

Lohat feels for Hansa. He has no fears of his own for his son because Lohat has remained in a state of grace. He had been broken by despair and collapsed in the woodland, but the sadhu appeared and gave him a promise. The couple would have a son who would be Vishnu incarnate. Lohat has since come to see that the sadhu was not simply a holy man but the very appearance of Vishnu. Jambho is still a young boy. It will take time for his body to adjust to containing Vishnu's force.

Yet Lohat understands how Hansa is consumed by a mother's fears. She did not encounter Vishnu in the guise of the sadhu. She cannot feel so secure.

Hansa asks around and hears of a tantric healer with supernatural powers who might expel whatever was hampering her son's progress. Isn't he worth a try? The healer is expensive, but Lohat sees his wife's need. He agrees to employ the healer and his array of assistants. What's more, he adds a bonus. Help Jambho speak like a normal child, he tells the healer, and Lohat will throw in the reward of a milk-yielding cow.

Preparations are extensive. The number 108 is sacred and so 108 earthenware lamps are stoked with linseed oil and wicks. A site is selected, a special platform is built for the rites, and the seven-year-old Jambho is placed in a central seat. Chants are sung. It is time to light the lamps.

And yet try as he might, the tantric healer cannot manage this simple task. The wicks might as well have been soaked in water. Touch the flame direct to the oil and the flame goes out. The lamps remain unlit and the onlookers start muttering.

Look at the boy, though. Something is happening. Usually Jambho is in some world of his own, and nothing you do makes him focus. But now he's watching. It's as if he's studying the scene. The healer and his assistants are running around, emptying lamps of their fuel, refilling them, desperate to make them light. Jambho gets to his feet and walks away. He comes back carrying an earthenware pitcher. The pitcher hasn't been fired, it won't be able to hold water, but of course Jambho won't know that. He ties a thin thread to its handle and lowers it down the well. At least he's trying, but that foolish boy, people think, for they know the pitcher won't hold the water and the thread is too thin to bear such weight.

Yet the pitcher fills with water and the thread holds as the water is pulled from the depths. Jambho carries the water to the lamps. He fills each vessel and wets the wicks. Foolish boy.

And then Jambho speaks and does so clearly.

'*Om*,' he says; the sacred word.

And with his word, each of the 108 lamps ignites.

The crowd knows they have witnessed a miracle.

'This is not the boy's doing,' the tantric healer tries. 'He is held in sway by a demon.'

The smile Jambho gives the healer is broad and pure. Those who see him smile are moved by wonder.[33]

This story is continued in the first of the hundred and twenty talks recorded from the guru's words, a collection known as the *shabads*, or 'statements'. The name Jambho now carries the suffix -ji which shows respect. In this first *shabad*, the seven-year-old Jambhoji delivers a powerful verse sermon in his Marwari language. He rebukes the healer as someone who profits from the dark arts. Those who invest belief in such figures should know better, he tells the villagers. It takes the Supreme Being to pull them out of their worldly desires. Instead of charlatans they should seek the true guru.

It's fair to wonder whether the seven-year-old found voice in verse in this way. Stories accrue within the lifetime of spiritual figures and myths take shape. An interesting aspect of Bishnoism is that the religion is still attached to its local roots. The events of Jambhoji's life turned much of what is now Rajasthan into a holy land, villagers passing tales down through the generations. In his birth town of Pipasar visitors can climb white stone steps and look down into the well where the seven-year-old Jambhoji drew water to fuel the oil lamps. And on a slope by the road at the edge of the town they will be shown a tree growing beside a bush.

The tree is a khejri and the bush that grows beside it is a kheer. We'll take a look at this combination of tree and shrub later: for now, the local story pinpoints this as the site of the next recorded incident in young Jambhoji's life.

A prince was passing through the village. His name was Rao Duda Jodhawat Rathod, and by rights he should be ruling the small kingdom of Merta. But his relatives had turned against him and chased him and his few loyal men over the borders of his homeland.

From his horse the prince looked across a field and spotted a young man tending a herd of cattle and a flock of goats.

He had brought them to a pond. Click went the young man's fingers, and the female goats moved forward to drink from the pond's edge while the males stayed back. Click again and the females withdrew, the males taking their place. Who was this man who controlled animals just by clicking his fingers?

The prince charged forward with his horse to find out. The young man moved away. He didn't seem to be running, but when the prince roused his horse to a gallop the young man became still more distant. Rao Duda climbed down from his horse: and now that he had stopped charging forward, he found the young man standing before him.

Beside this very khejri tree and the kheer bush on the outskirts of Pipasar.

With one direct look from the young man's eyes the prince sensed in himself why these animals were so tuned to the young man's wishes. There was no separation. This man, who was Jambhoji, was not imposing his will but was instead alert to the needs of others.

Rao Duda explained his predicament, his exile, how he feared he and his men would never be allowed to return to his kingdom.

Jambhoji reached into the kheer shrub and brought out a slender branch. 'Carry this stick,' he told the prince. 'But carry it like a sword and it will be like a sword. Go back to Merta. Your kingdom will be yours again.'

Jambhoji returned to his herd and his flock. Rao Duda turned back to Merta, wielding his stick as he might a sword. While still beyond the borders of his kingdom he met a crowd of his people coming to find him. They needed him to return and take control.

And so he did. Jambhoji's direction had come true.

The image of Jambhoji with his long white hair and beard, his saffron robes and conical hat, is portrayed in every Bishnoi shrine. Yet perhaps it is invented. 'Guru Jambhoji said to one of his disciples "Nobody knows what I look like," a Bishnoi priest told me. '"They don't even know if I am a man or a woman."' He spurned children of his own, informing his parents that he would never marry.

Then in 1483, when Jambhoji was thirty-two, his father died. A few months later his mother died too. Jambhoji became a landowner. He no more wanted that than to marry. Freed of obligation to his parents, Jambhoji walked away from the family property. His journey took him six miles to the top of a high, fixed dune. This hill of sand, known as Samrathal, was now his home. It was a good time to leave farming behind. That year's monsoon rains failed, as did the next, and a profound ten-year drought hit the region.

Jambhoji sat on his hilltop in the shade of a tree, closed inside the profound bliss of meditation. But like the Buddha under a bodhi tree, and Muhammad in his cave retreat, there was no surviving in bliss while the world suffered. 'I am in everything,' Jambhoji once said, 'and everything is in me.' There is no separation between the world and himself; if the world is sick, then he is sick. And he needs to find a cure.

6

How to Live in a Megadrought

JOIN ME WITHIN THE SHADE OF A KANKERI TREE. It's not the tallest of trees but it's an evergreen and its canopy is broad; there's room for a group of friends to enjoy the shade. It's July. Outside the tree's shadow it is hot, 37 degrees Celsius. We have a clear view of a new Bishnoi temple with its sandstone cupola, but it is acres of white marble flagstones away. Take off your sandals to cross that marble and you'd be hopping foot to foot.

It could have been worse. The official definition of an Indian heatwave is a daily temperature over 45°C, and this summer of 2022 Rajasthan has experienced twenty-four such days. India has seen five times more heatwaves than the year before. Yet on this July day while we shelter from India's heat, planes are being diverted from London's Heathrow Airport because its runways are melting. Rajasthan is hot but London is hotter. Today, for the first time in recorded history, the temperature in Britain breaks the 40°C barrier (104°F). And all-time high temperatures are recorded across the globe. Wichita Falls in Texas smashed through a record set in 2018, reaching 46°C (115°F). A hundred and thirty weather stations in China matched or beat historic record highs.

This kankeri we're sheltered beneath is one of those desert trees that winds its roots deep down through dry earth. 'Trees are for all', as the schoolboy taught me, and this one has been growing here for more than five hundred years. The 1530s was a decade in which heat and drought hit historic highs. This place is Lalasar, an hour's ride in a bullock cart from where Guru Jambhoji lived most of his life, and in the 1530s he was in his eighties, yet he made the journey to move here. What attracted him?

'It's so beautiful,' a Lalasar temple priest told me, waving a hand to take in distant horizons over flat land marked green by desert scrub. 'And the climate is famous. It is mild. There is always a pleasant breeze.'

Maybe so.

Jambhoji would not leave here alive. This kankeri tree is sacred so nobody is going to drill a hole through its gnarled trunk. If they did, it would reveal its history. We humans, even in the year we die of old age, keep sloughing off skin and growing new layers. Trees do the same, even in years when added girth is barely skin thick. Studies of annual tree rings in ancient trees show that droughts of the sixteenth-century spanned the globe. Climates can swing between extremes, maybe damp one year and dry the next, but David Stahle, Professor of Geosciences at the University of Arkansas, examined North American tree ring records and noted that in the 1500s 'the basement collapsed and went down to another level'.[34] This was the most sustained drought in a thousand years.

In Europe this decade of drought years in the 1530s led to the 1540 megadrought, when the rivers Elbe, Rhine and Seine were so shallow that people waded across them, and the Thames ran so low that the sea poured in to change the river's direction. Fields dried and split with cracks so deep they could swallow a leg. Fires consumed forests and houses, and the German town of Einbeck turned to ashes in a matter of hours. Looking for scapegoats, authorities turned on their religious opponents and on climate refugees, torturing them to obtain confessions of arson.[35]

How does that distant epoch experienced by Jambhoji compare to now? As we sit beneath this tree in Lalasar in July 2022, the year has months to run. Yet at the beginning of August, Andrea Toreti, a senior researcher with the European Commission's Joint Research Centre, will call a press conference. Nothing had eclipsed that 1540 megadrought until 2018. And now, as in the 1530s, one bad year presaged worse. Worse was 2022. '1540 is a very famous event,' he announced, 'and if we look back over the last 500 years, it is the only one that gets close ... in terms of severity.'[36]

The worst drought in five hundred years? That bad?

Worse.

Using data collected in Europe, other scientists announced that the run of summer droughts, suddenly intensifying in 2015, was the worst in over two millennia. 'Climate change does not mean that it will get drier everywhere,' the paper's lead author, Ulf Buntgen of Cambridge University, explained. 'Some places may get wetter or colder, but extreme conditions will become more frequent, which could be devastating for agriculture, ecosystems and societies as a whole.'[37]

That July I passed through one hot, dry Rajasthani village. Three days later, after fierce monsoon rains, two children who lived there were swept to their deaths by flood. I became marooned in my Jodhpur city hotel while the roads around me turned into rivers. And in August 2022, a few hundred miles to the west, a third of Pakistan would be covered by floodwaters.

In November 1535, aged eighty-five, Guru Jambhoji laid himself down beneath this kankeri tree and passed away. He was born into a desert region set to be challenged by unprecedented droughts, and left teachings as to how his people could survive. Do those teachings apply to the world, now?

United Nations experts say that a billion people in a hundred countries face their homelands turning to desert. The all-time record highs experienced in Rajasthan in 2022 were once seen as being part of a three-hundred-year cycle. Now they are expected every three years.

Bishnois explained to me that Guru Jambhoji was an early environmental scientist, but because villagers of fifteenth- and sixteenth-century India weren't open to scientific discourse he couched his teachings in religious terms. He taught lessons of sustainable living that we are starting to learn and apply now.[38]

He was prescient in that way, but you'll find that the teachings go deeper than that. 'Keep body and mind pure,' Jambhoji would teach his followers. 'Be restrained, and do not let happiness perish. As the world criticises you, keep fulfilling your duties. Avoid attractive women just as deer run away from the vibrating sound of a bow.'

In 1483, on his parents' deaths, Jambhoji walked away from farming duties to his sand dune retreat. A kankeri tree, such as the one he would die beneath, grew near its top and Jambhoji settled beneath its shade.

It's usual in India for holy men to set themselves apart on hillsides and the flanks of mountains. There's something aspirational about the move, rising above the earthly plain. The main thrust for Jambhoji was to move beyond worldly concerns.

Reflecting on his farming years and his time of wealth, he said: 'Mist starts falling during the night, the sun spreads its heat during the day, wind flows cold and hot, and clouds make heavy rains. Worldly people wake up with a concern for farming when water starts falling down. However some fools do not wake up even then. On the body on which I now wear woollen clothes, I used to wear soft clothes. The hands by which I now turn the rosary for chanting, I used to count diamonds.'

Because of the drought, families were fleeing their villages and moving to land that might not be parched. They would slaughter any blackbuck and chinkara that drew near, and chop down trees for fuel to cook them with.

Much of Jambhoji's teaching focuses on the inevitability of death. 'This body is perishable,' he reminds emperors and yogis. 'It is born and it perishes. Those who do not know the creation and destruction of the body are ignorant.'

On the desert plains below Jambhoji's sand dune retreat, camels stretched their necks into empty stone troughs where

they found nothing to drink and now lay dead. The people down there did not need reminding.

'The kankeri tree is my temple,' Jambhoji told his people, 'And my dwelling.'

It's 1485. People sit on the summit of the sand dune and watch Jambhoji as he sits within the shade cast by the small kankeri tree. And as they watch, the shade vanishes, consumed by an orb of intense white light that surrounds the desert mystic. Quite likely their hearts hammered fast inside their chests. Perhaps they stared for a while, amazed, and then turned to each other. What should they do? Leave him be, they decide ... keep watch.

'I have neither shadow, nor illusion, nor flesh, nor any other bodily elements,' he will later say. 'I am self-illuminated. Nobody knows my beginning. Worldly people merely have a hazy guess about me. I am caretaker of everything and a supporter of all like a reflection in the water – as the sun reflects in the water I also reflect in the world.'

Jambhoji was turned inward, a figure unified with his god, complicit in timeless acts of creation. 'I have obtained Him,' he would say, 'by devotion and continuous chanting.'

He did not want the lessons that his god, Vishnu, was gifting him, because they required a return to the world he had left.

And yet his people were suffering.

His revelation showed him the root of that suffering.

At its simplest, people had to stop living in conflict with their environment. They had to cease their war with the natural world, killing its trees and its animals and fleeing as though the climate was a conquering army. They had to live in harmony with the natural world.

But how?

He came down from his hill. He set out his teachings.

The headline about Bishnoism, setting it apart from other religions, is its specific focus on conserving wildlife and nature.* Jambhoji's teachings were codified into twenty-nine rules. In his local language of Marwari, *bish* translates as twenty, and *noi* as nine: these twenty-nine rules are so central to Bishnoi life that they name the religion. A third of these rules focus on people's relationship with creatures and plants of the natural world.†

Chief among these is the instruction to 'be kind to all living beings'. If you're a man, would you like to be castrated? Then don't castrate bulls. 'If you're pricked by a thorn, the pain is intolerable,' Jambhoji pointed out. 'Do you imagine pain is different for an animal?'

Never kill an animal. And never cut a branch from a green tree in which the sap still flows.

In human terms: don't lie, or speak about those who are not there, or argue for arguments sake; be forgiving and show compassion; hold your baser instincts in check; before doing anything else in the morning, wash yourself.

Rules on spiritual practice say how to perform the daily fire ritual, and advocate chanting the name of Vishnu.[39] Jambhoji

---

* Jains also adhere to deep ecological principles, though scholars question whether such principles form the purpose of their religion. For more on this, see p.207.

† For a list and explanation of the twenty-nine rules, see the Appendix.

told his followers: 'Recite the name of Vishnu. The majority of people meet failure because their worship is motivated by worldly needs. Pure worship is done only by a few. One is not free from the cycle of transmigration without the true and selfless worship of Vishnu. Remember him always, this alone is the key to success.'

Despite the divine origin of these teachings, applying them could not end drought overnight.

So Jambhoji offered direct help.

Jambhoji used his family's funds to buy in grain. Villagers were free to come and take the grain they needed to feed their household. In exchange they had to make one promise: not to harm or kill any animal.[40]

Jambhoji also bought seed from neighbouring states, and he paid for camels to transport it. Villagers could use this seed to plant their fields and believe in a future.

The store of Jambhoji's grain, they say, had a miraculous quality of replenishing itself. However many came to take their food from it, enough remained for others.

The camels that transported the seed, they say, walked in a cloud of their own fragrance. In the excitement of offloading the seed the villagers forgot to keep an eye on the camels. When they came to look for them, the animals had vanished. The villagers could find no footprints nor any signs that showed which way the camels had gone.

'Having read the Vedas and Koran,' Jambhoji the practical man would say, 'people have only created confusions and myths have engulfed them.'

Perhaps there's a difference between myths and miracles. At the opening of this chapter, I asked you to join me beneath a sacred kankeri tree in the temple of Lalasar, enjoying its shade. Before we leave this temple of Lalasar, look around for a moment. A flag flutters over a tomb in the distant temple grounds, where the previous much-loved high priest, Swami Rajendarand, is buried.[41] He died the year before from Covid. And sitting cross-legged on a daybed in a covered walkway is Ram Das, a man in priestly saffron.

Five years ago, Ram Das was in a hospital bed in Bikaner, the nearest city. He had cancer, his stomach riddled with multiple tumours. The doctors had battled to save him, but it was no use. The battle was lost, they declared. They would stop treatment and let Ram Das die.

The high priest Rajendarand grew angry. From beneath the kankeri tree where we took shelter, under which Jambhoji had died, he sent Jambhoji a demand. 'This man is dying and in great pain. If you have any power, show it to us! Otherwise, why have we been sitting here all these years?'

Ram Das sits utterly still, quite thin, his grey beard and grey hair rimming a face dominated by a pair of large glasses with transparent frames. It is as though being alive still surprises him. He tells how he very soon felt better. Ten days after the high priest shouted his demand at Jambhoji, Ram Das was up and walking. Here he is now, his cancer in full remission.

If a man can be saved from certain death, maybe there's still hope for our planet.

And hope for a giant bird on the edge of extinction. Let's cross the Thar Desert and go see.

7

In the Land of the Great Indian Bustard

THE BISHNOI GUESTHOUSE is at the edge of town, with modern cabins at the rear. Beyond is desert. The Thar Desert covers five per cent of India's land mass and reaches into Pakistan, so its terrain varies with the geology. You'll find desert canyon lands, and sixty miles to the west of here, on the border with Pakistan, tourists take camel trains into steep dunes of white and shifting sand. Those are romantic desert landscapes. The one ahead of me isn't, but it's how most deserts look: sheer expanse of open views, baked ground strewn with rocks, tufts of grasses a dusty green above sand, thorny shrubs and occasional twisted trees.

Despite the emptiness, the Thar is the least deserted desert in the world. The Bishnoi have had a lot to do with that, having worked out how to farm there. Each square mile of this desert holds an average of eighty people.

But we're not looking for people.

Radheshyam Bishnoi, from the local village of Dholia, is my guide. He's in his twenties and makes a good poster child for Bishnoi activism. On his Facebook page he holds a chinkara against his chest, young man rivalling gazelle for the quality of their cheekbones, soulful eyes and long eyelashes.

As an infant, Radheshyam's heart went out to the chinkara. He could pick up one of these little gazelles, nuzzle nose to nose, press its warmth against his chest and feel its heart beating. As a teenager he began to act like the animals' older brother. At dawn the animals came to the edge of his village to feed. If ever one didn't show, he went in search of it.

In this way, he came to know their habitat. Sometimes he would carry a sick chinkara home and nurse it to health. But some were injured, with gaping wounds from dog bites. They needed more expert help.

Radheshyam would take the overnight bus to Jodhpur and the animal rescue centre attached to Jodhpur Zoo. Here he learned new techniques: tricks to help locate sick chinkara, who seek hiding places where they can try to recover; symptoms you can spot and so shape your diagnosis; emergency treatments you can give; dressings to apply and food supplements to boost their systems. Decide how best to carry the wounded creatures, in your arms or over your shoulder. If an animal needs a surgeon, then get back on the overnight bus to Jodhpur Zoo and bring it with you. In his teenage years, Radheshyam rescued almost five hundred chinkara.

With their large ears, chinkara hear danger and then run. Their hooves kick up plumes of dust. With eyes in the side of your head, you'd be able to scan the breadth of desert for such plumes, and the kicked-up dust of a fleeing chinkara would serve as your alarm call. Luckily for one giant bird, they have such eyes. For millions of years, way before primates evolved into humans, they used this lateral vision to thrive in desert lands. This is the Great Indian Bustard, the State bird of Rajasthan. It's over three foot tall and weighs forty pounds, about as big as a bird can be and still be able to take wing. A bird that big should be easy to find.

Then people came and built wind turbines, and cables between tall pylons to ferry to the city electricity garnered from desert winds.

Now the species is almost extinct.

Hence my need for a guide.

It's two hours before dusk. Radheshyam steers his jeep off the road and speeds across the desert. Way across to our left we see the desert dust plume kicked up by the hooves of a racing chinkara. Radheshyam's neck tautens and there's a quick shift of his head to the left. The jeep brakes and he leaps out.

'Come come,' he breathes, beckoning with his hand. I leave the door ajar to avoid any noise. My binoculars show me desert trees and shrubs and grasses and sand and nothing more and I feel foolish and desperate but Radheshyam wheels his hand in the air, further, look further, and I do, and YES!

The bird's neck is straight, its head making short fractional moves as it scans a far horizon. It spotted the chinkara dust. It will have seen us, its eyes are keen, but we're keeping still and distant and are no direct threat. It starts to walk.

Scanning wide through my binoculars brings five birds into view. They move in a line, and their steady progress is reminiscent of the flat and wet lands of East Yorkshire where boats in thin rivers can seem to be sailing through fields. These bustards are stately.

This is a group of five males. Their bodies are brown, their necks white, with black crowns to their heads. Here the desert has a covering of tall dry grasses and the birds dip their beaks to pick out seeds, insects and spiders. It takes multiple grains and pinches of animal protein to feed a bird this big so they waste no energy. Step step, pause a while, scan the desert, dip their beaks to the dirt, swallow down a morsel, step step. As a species we humans are arrivistes; the fossil record shows bustards have been working the globe for around thirty million years. They have stepped out from a time when humans did not trammel the earth.

Our jeep has been following a rough route laid down by previous tyre tracks, but now we speed along a road of compacted sand that passes between two pylons. When evening approaches the bustards use this track as a flyway, moving from their feeding ground to their water source. Because Great Indian Bustards are so heavy, their flight is low. Because their eyes are in the sides of their heads, they don't see the powerlines that are stretched across the flyway and so crash into them. Every year, between ten and twenty of these bustards are electrocuted in this way.

How many of this species of bird survive? Fewer than one hundred and fifty. Which means that ten per cent of the global population are killed by powerlines every year. It's a major reason why Great Indian Bustards are hurtling toward extinction.

A bustard once flew into these lines above us. Radheshyam found its body on the ground. Inform the officials of such an accidental death and they will send along a junior officer to bury the carcase. Radheshyam made that call, but first he rang his Bishnoi friends. They came and stood guard over the bird's body and wouldn't let it be buried. That would no longer do. Instead, the authorities were told they had to fit a reflector, a 'diverter', to the wires, which flashes sunlight by day and stores solar energy so as to emit LED signals at night. The bustards have more of a chance of seeing these flashing lights than the thin strips of electric wire.

Radheshyam climbed a transmission tower to stand at the height of the wires. A junior officer duly arrived at the scene. This man encountered the Bishnoi guard standing around the bustard's corpse. He looked up to find Radheshyam clinging to the pylon's steel. 'Fit a reflector,' Radheshyam yelled down. 'Or I will jump.'

Radheshyam's life for a bustard; it was a cheap price to pay.

This was above the officer's pay grade. He got on the phone. They had a group of Bishnois to deal with. One was on top of a transmission tower, threatening to jump.

The forestry department doesn't take Bishnoi threats lightly. They sent along a high official. Radheshyam's demand stayed the same. Fit a reflector or he would jump.

Radheshyam is still with us. And reflectors now glint from the wires.

The sun's dropping. It's time for birds to roost and men to head home – unless you're a man who likes to steal out at night.

Our jeep pauses when a man on a motorbike, a white turban for his helmet, flags us down. He's just spotted a likely poacher. Radheshyam pulls out his phone and relays the news to others. His patrol patch covers seven thousand acres, but he'll rush to investigate reports of incidents in an area sixty miles by fifty. Radheshyam's reach is broadened by men like this turbaned motorcyclist who is on his way home. Cattle and camel herders are also out there, shepherds, farm labourers, and each has a phone. Each cares for this environment. When they spot something that disrupts it, they call Radheshyam, who relays the news to others in his Bishnoi group or deals with it himself. He's at the centre of a whole web of informants.

'Look,' Radheshyam says, turning his phone so I can see its screen.

This scene is from ten days ago, a bustard flapping its broad dark wings at the air. Fruitlessly. Its feet are caught in a barbed wire fence. The clip ends and Radheshyam presses to start it again, the bird trapped in a flapping loop. Ultimately this phone is what freed it. The phone had rung. One of Radheshyam's network of informants had spotted the bird and called him. Radheshyam raced to the fence and the rescue. That Great Indian Bustard, close to one per cent of the surviving population, was gathered into Radheshyam's arms for a while, its feet disentangled from the wire, and then let free.

Guiding tourists suits Radheshyam, because he will be out keeping an eye on the desert in any case, and it provides a little income. Radheshyam's fellow villagers make some money from running a dairy business and sometimes help Radheshyam out when he needs funds for his wildlife rescue work, but essentially he is a volunteer. Couldn't he join the forestry department?

He doesn't have the qualifications. And besides ... 'What I'm doing is on top of what I could do there. I would only replace someone else. What I do is over and above.'

He's part of the All India Wildlife Protection Bishnoi Support – one of several groups akin to the Bishnoi Tiger Force. They do thirty to forty per cent of the forestry department's work, he says, because when officials in their offices receive alerts it's the Bishnoi who are out in the field. The officials reach for their phones and the Bishnoi spring into action

In any event, a formal job would mean following orders. The call of bureaucracy would replace the call of the desert. Radheshyam knows he's more effective because he's not just doing a job. 'It's my passion in life.'

Root around any significant Indian hill and you'll likely find a holy man. Tricuta, a rocky hill of sheer sides and three peaks, rises out of the Thar Desert. Back in the twelfth century it was home to Eesul, a desert hermit known for telling the future. One day a renegade prince, Prince Jaisal, climbed up to ask his counsel. Eesul told him how Lord Krishna had once declared that just such a prince as Jaisal would rule from this hilltop. But beware. Any fort built here would be sacked at least twice.

Jaisal built his hilltop fortress and so Tricuta became Jaisalmer, the rock of Jaisal. The fortress was indeed besieged, three times, and then Jaisalmer found fortune as a trading post on the overland spice route. In the eighteenth century new seaports opened 650 miles south in Mumbai, which diverted trade from the bandit-ridden overland route. The hilltop town is now a medieval treasureland: delicate latticework of sandstone, carved friezes, doorways festooned with ancient iron, cupolas and archways and slabbed and narrow winding streets.

The fortress city and the vertical flanks of its hilly base shine pink in the morning light, but not yet. It's still dark. The highway beyond it leads to Sam, a low-slung trading town that straddles the desert road. Inside one of a run of single-storey buildings is the research station of the Wildlife Institute of India.[42]

It's 6am. Young scientists are still cocooned in their sleeping bags on the concrete floors. They rouse themselves. Four soon join me in their jeep, their sleep a victim of their research: birds don't sleep in.

Nor do birds like empty sand dunes. Imagine desert and you'll probably come up with scenes like those due west of here, where tourists have been sleeping in desert camps for views of starlit skies. They'll rise early too, keen to avoid the hottest slice of day, and mount camels that will carry them up and down over the sandy hills.

Our jeep races east, back toward Jaisalmer, and then veers off-road. Blackness lifts and the desert floor picks up its subtle variation of colours, pale sand, grey rocks, brown grasses, dusty green shrubs, and then the red orb of sun rising through a veil of mist to pink the whole sky.

A sudden burst of speed rivals the jeep's. These are antelopes, a large species known as nilgai, which translates as 'blue bull'. The name comes from the heft and the dark colouring of the males, but these beasts are tawny brown females with their young. They can run at thirty miles an hour, which is what they do now, trailing dust clouds till they're specks.

What are they doing here? Blackbucks are the antelopes who are adapted to desert living, but even so you won't find them in this tough region of the desert. Nilgai have migrated in because this section of desert is farmed. They can leap six-foot high fences and love to munch down crops. The Bishnoi tithe what they produce, are happy to give a tenth of their grain to feed wildlife, but since nilgai can snaffle down a tenth of their crops without asking they see it as fair to shout and chase them away.

What's it like, then, for these farmers to share their land with giant birds? Finding the answer to that question is why the scientists come this way at dawn: Great Indian Bustards shun dry dunes and share with farmers those desert areas where plants can grow. They're pecking through grasses, taking seeds and beetles and other morsels. The previous week they were able to be gluttons, for thick clouds of locusts passed through to ravage the desert.

We're driving fast because the scientists already have their sighting: the location of a Great Indian Bustard is showing up on their phones. They are anxious to get to a viewing point so they can study the bird in its habitat before it walks or flies away. The bird is a female. On an earlier trip they had set a trap. They knew that at some point every day she would go to a watering hole. Her normal gait sees her dragging her feet, and so across her path to the water they stretched nylon loops between bamboo sticks. On her way for her morning drink her feet caught in the nylon. Scientists dashed out of their hiding place to hold her still, fixed a transmitter to her body and then let her go. Since then the transmitter's signal tells them where she is.

Of course, after being snagged like that she's now more wary of humans. The bird is best watched from afar. Occasional rocky outcrops, known as *mugarra*, stud this land. We head for one. It's thirty feet high. We park so the *mugarra* hides the jeep and climb to look out from the hill's far side.

The scientists, men in their twenties and early thirties and one young woman, Tanya Gupta, are here to witness early morning bustard behaviour. Their eyes are keen and they find their target female in a group of three – two females and a male. Quickly fitting a spotting scope to its tripod they bring the trio up close. The birds are feeding and so exact coordinates of the grass clumps they reach their beaks into, the shrubs they peck from, are noted down. There's an arachnologist on the team. When the birds move on he'll rush down there and scrutinise the ground. Hopefully the bustards found and ate some spiders from this patch, but not all of them. He'll find the ones they missed and note down the species. The spiders will be added to their list of items that form bustard diet in this favoured habitat.

There's sudden excitement, the scientists lining up by the spotting scope's eyepiece. It's February, it's chilly, not the season for mating, but something has roused the male. Maybe that locust boost to his diet last week. From below his beak and down his long throat runs a stretch of featherless skin. He's filled it with air, ballooning it into a mighty white jowl, and is starting to strut. This is lekking, the male moving into display mode to set female hearts aflutter.

Not today, mate. The female pair barely glance sideways and continue to peck at the ground. And at a distance to the right two male farmers, clad in Bishnoi white, are heading their way.

Devendra Pandey, the tallest of the team, in his baseball cap and with his soft black beard and ready smile, is watching the two men. 'Protected areas without humans is a nonsense,' he tells me. 'The birds love the human areas and have no problem with the farmers.'

Each of these scientists has a specialty and Devendra's is feral dogs. Nothing grows on this land in winter, people leave till monsoon rains return, but the dogs stay. They hunt chinkara, sometimes for food but more often because it's fun to hunt. Bustards lay their eggs on open ground and dogs find them tasty. He tells me a lot about dogs.

'Do you empathise with them?' I ask. 'Does your work lead you to think like a dog?'

He resists, keeps explaining how they destroy the ecological balance, how much more damaging they are than the wolves that once roamed these areas – but then he grows silent and looks into the distance and smiles and says, 'If I were a dog I would be cunning. Dogs are cunning. Three will hide in shrubs and two will herd the chinkara toward them. Then they all pounce and take it down.'

Devendra studied zoology in Mumbai. 'I couldn't bear to go back to a city,' he says, and breaks off. The male bustard has deflated his pouch, the females have stopped eating. They'll have seen the two farmers long ago, and far away was OK, but closer? How large is a bustard's comfort zone? How close can humans come? The scientists measure the distance between men and birds, the farmers keep walking forward ... that close! The trio of birds start running, they beat their wings, they launch into low flight.

The farmers turn their heads to watch them go. Later the scientists will take what they have learned down to the community. How many insects does it take to fuel a bustard's flight? Quite a few. The farmers know about marginal existence. If they know how close they can come to the birds, perhaps they'll come no closer. These are Bishnoi farmers. They know they don't own this land, but co-habit it. Already they've agreed to fence off fields of grass where these great Indian bustards can safely lay their eggs.

One person charged with taking the science down to local schools and villages is Tanya Gupta. She's up here now and smiling brightly. 'Becoming liked is the first step,' she says. 'Some see advantages for birds, others need to be incentivised.'

The slogan 'Bustard Recovery' is splashed across her T-shirt. For four years, in Jaipur, she had worked with Raksha, 'Voice of the Voiceless', a youth-based organisation that runs twenty-four-hour helplines for birds and animals that need to be rescued. 'I always wanted to do something for animals and birds because they can't speak for themselves. If we don't do anything they are doomed to die.'

Here's the curious things about these young scientists, bunking down on concrete floors and heading into the desert at dawn. They see doom coming and find purpose in fighting it. Down by their headquarters in Sam is a fenced-off compound. It holds nine Great Indian Bustard chicks, the first batch born from eggs these scientists found out in the wild. The chicks have names. One, Toni, hatched on the day the writer Toni Morrison died. 'I'm a foster mother of some of the chicks.' Tanya's eyes shine. 'It's an awesome thing to do. We get to massage birds and play with them. This is the founder population, so we have to connect with the birds.'

They have four generations in which to do this work. If this isn't to stay a captive population, that fourth generation will grow up without human contact and must be released. Into what?

This is the purpose of these scientists' research. Soon, if their fears come to pass, Great Indian Bustards will become extinct in the wild. What does 'wild' mean to these birds? What is the habitat that sustains them? This remnant population of wild bustards is showing survival skills they've picked up over thirty million years. The scientists are picking up that knowledge. The clock is set and the timer is running. They have so many years to restore this desert habitat into one where their captive bustards can step out and thrive.

It's breakfast time. Tubs of pot noodles appear, along with the project's director Dr Sutirtha Dutta, in his thirties, dressed for the morning chill in his green Marmot windcheater. It took a Masters degree on the spine-tailed lizard to bring him from his birth city of Calcutta to this desert, and then any excuse to keep him here. His PhD topic was the Great Indian Bustard. 'The landscape can seem monotonous to some people,' he says, looking out through brown oblong glasses, 'but it's thrilling to have visibility up to the horizon.'

The near horizon is marked by a giant wind turbine; the trio of bustards had been feeding at its base. 'This,' and Sutirtha gestures with his hand, 'is viewed as unproductive land – the term used is 'wasteland'. The dominant discourse is on how to change these lands to agricultural use, more

productive for human life. The current plan is to adapt the land for renewable energy.'

Hence the wind turbines. Hence those overhead power-lines. Sutirtha and a colleague spent a year going up and down a sixty-mile stretch of these power lines. From beneath the wires they picked up bird carcases from a variety of species before the bodies could decompose. Each month, from each mile, they retrieved five. That amounts to those wires killing a hundred thousand birds from tiny species to large every year. Their next task is to collect carcases from beneath the wind turbines' blades.

What needs to happen if these birds are to survive out here?

'Land now regarded as wasteland has to be appreciated as unique and valuable habitat, and therefore protected.'

In the desert on the far side of Jaisalmer the population of Great Indian Bustards, those in Radheshyam's care, is increasing. Here, in the area monitored by the scientists, their numbers are going down. How come?

A few years back the Bishnoi weren't bothering to look out for these birds, Sutirtha counters. Also a military zone is adjacent to Bishnoi land, which is a perfect undisturbed area. The scientists help out the Bishnoi – it was Sutirtha's project that supplied the two hundred diverters they wanted for the overhead power lines – but scientists have a different approach. 'The Bishnoi are species-centric. Carnivores – foxes, wolves and dogs – they're all seen as villains,' says Sutirtha, implying that the Bishnoi protect other animals from carnivores, by building a fence perhaps, and so disrupting the ecological balance that requires carnivores to eat. 'Theirs is not a scientific form of conservation, but it has served many conservation purposes.'

He thinks more and then brightens. He has recalled another significant innovation from these Bishnoi conservation activists: Radheshyam on his phone to the camel herders, the shepherds, the labourers, who all feed back environmental alerts from over a wide territory – a vigilance network, Sutirtha terms it. 'The vigilance network is absolutely amazing,' he says and smiles, his eyes shining, 'and worth replicating.'

In the 1970s, twelve hundred Great Indian Bustards lived in the wild. That number has crashed by nearly ninety per cent. Conservation breeding is an insurance policy. Perhaps fifteen years from now, the young of the breeding population will be returned to the wild. The world has that long to ensure they have a survivable habitat. 'The philosophy is to buy time.'

Are the Bishnoi species-specific in their conservation stances, as Sutirtha claims? I will keep finding evidence that refutes it. Back in Dholia, Radheshyam shows me photographs of desert foxes, victims of sarcoptic mange that sees mites burrowing under their skin so that their hair drops out. He wrote to Rajasthan's chief wildlife warden, demanding action.

And on a dawn trip, Radheshyam takes me to some other carnivores. Breeze-block cattle sheds mark the edge of his village. Beyond, the bumpy ground of shrubs and khejri is too harsh to farm. When cattle die in the area, here is where some of their carcases are brought.

It's early, the sun is giving more light than heat, and vultures are congregating. One dominates the scene; four-foot-tall, high on a mound, black as a priest, stands a cinereous vulture whose outspread wings can stretch up to ten feet. The main crowd, scores of them and greyer than their name, are Indian white-backed vultures. They are social creatures who can soar close to ten thousand feet and fly at 50mph, but not after eating. They favour the soft flesh by a carcase's tail. They'll flap and fight with each other and gorge until they are so heavy they are flightless.

The third species in this morning assembly is a Eurasian griffon, its wings adding a golden sheen to the mix. Their eyesight is so keen they can spot a carcase from three miles away. Nearby cattle carcases still have flesh on them but the air is chilled. These vultures gather like parliamentarians in the lobby, warming themselves before breakfast.

Seven vulture species make their homes in the Thar Desert. The king, Egyptian, long-billed and white-backed vultures all breed here while the Eurasian and Himalayan griffons and the cinereous vulture are winter visitors. In the past four years Radheshyam has rescued almost sixty of these birds. Many are made sick by eating carcases that have been poisoned by people who want to rid their land of scavengers, and into these vultures he injects the anti-poisoning medication atropine.

Trains on the rail line that runs through the Thar Desert strike animals, leaving behind a trail of dead creatures that vultures then drop in to eat. With your head dug into a corpse to enjoy a feast like that, you tend not to notice trains roaring in behind you. Over a two-year period, a hundred and fifty vultures were killed by such train strikes. Radheshyam brought his phone network onto high alert to help him monitor the tracks. When anyone spots a dead animal carcase on the railway tracks they call, and Radheshyam or his friends will drive fast and drag the carcase clear. The vultures can then feast in safety.

The number of vultures killed by trains since this monitoring started? Zero.

From the vultures, Radheshyam takes me to meet his mentor. It is still early, because the man we seek has to go to work for the forestry department. Kamlesh Bishnoi is small, sturdy and dark-complexioned, wearing a woolly hat emblazoned with '76, which I assume to be his year of birth since he is in his forties. We sit on the mattress-free cot bed in his room and he brings us tea.

I know how the Bishnoi care for their wildlife, but what prompted Kamlesh to leave the normal rounds of village life and devote himself to conservation?

'I was driving a Russian tourist,' he says. 'We saw an injured desert cat on the road. The Russian made me stop and he got out of the car and picked up the creature and broke into tears. I was amazed. We the Bishnoi are meant to be the people who care for animals but this stranger is doing so much more than us. I knew I must do more.'

Suddenly things that Kamlesh had accepted as the way of life in the desert now upset him and called him to action. Chinkara only give birth to one young a year, and it takes a baby chinkara a day or two before it can walk. Kamlesh keeps an eye out for these births, but so do feral pigs, eager for an easy meal. Kamlesh chases the pigs away till the chinkara fawn is up on its feet.

When villagers build fences around their crops, he tells them how dangerous this is for the bustards, who tend to get entangled in the fence's barbed wire. Great Indian Bustards lay single eggs, a mottled brown, in shallow dips in the ground, and he does all he can to protect their nesting sites.

Further west, I'd seen how the Wildlife Institute of India had thirty scientists to deploy in the desert and find the nine eggs for their incubators. Here there is just Kamlesh and Radheshyam. When they do find an egg, Kamlesh pitches a small tent so he has a clear view of the nesting bustard. Bustards spend twenty-eight days incubating their eggs, and Kamlesh spends all those days on site, watching. After dark he reckons the bird and her egg are safe, so he goes home for some sleep, to be back by four the next morning. Only when the chick is hatched, and tucked safely beneath the apron of its mother's feathers, does Kamlesh end his vigil.

I have heard a lot about how the forestry department is weighed down by bureaucracy. Can he be effective there?

'I hope to be able to change the ways of the officials,' he says. 'And I only work for them eight out of the twenty-four hours. That leaves me the rest of the time to do my own work.'

Kamlesh's room is bare of possessions. The shepherds and camel herders and other informants in their vigilance network, who use their smartphones to call in sightings of poachers or animals in distress, are often not Bishnoi and don't have as keen a sense of protecting wildlife. It helps that he pays them a little of his salary, or uses it to buy them gifts such as flashlights.

'You saw five Great Indian Bustards here!' he declares and he smiles. 'Two or three years ago there were just two or three birds in this area, and now there are thirty. Many have flown in. When they are under threat they go about singly but now they have started to move in groups. You saw five. That is good. Very good. I have seen groups of ten and eleven. They feel safe here. We are making our desert a safe place.'

8

In the Animal Sanctuary

YOU'RE A YOUNG WOMAN, training to be a schoolteacher, and you know that the desert isn't a safe place. It's OK for you, that's not the problem, your safety isn't the issue. It's what happens to desert animals that melts your heart.

Take chinkara, those miniature gazelles with their soulful eyes and fragile legs. Deserts can be tough but chinkara have existed in this desert for seven million years. They browse pods, seeds and leaves from a range of sixty-three desert shrubs. In the heat of June when much is dry they munch at the shrub *Crotalaria burhia*, a bushy tangle of thin twigs. But in July, with the desert lands – the Bishnoi heartland near where Jambhoji grew up – replenished by monsoon rains, they can graze their fill on grasses and flowers.

Those were the old days. In the twenty-first century, as traffic streams to and from the trading town of Nokha, there are new dangers.

Here's the first: chinkara have not learned how to run from motorbikes and trucks. They keep getting struck when crossing roads. Then, when they're crossing fields, low-strung and electric fences that protect crops act as trip wires for fleeing chinkara. What are they fleeing?

Dogs. An estimated thirty-five million dogs free-roam India, many of them feral, dogs born in the world with no human interaction. The problem and number of these dogs is getting worse. In 2023 a quarter more Indians reported dog bites than in the previous year. And dogs are the biggest killers of chinkara. Surveys show that chinkara numbers in Rajasthan fell from 47,640 in 2018 to 41,412 in 2020.[43]

Add monsoon rains to those feral dogs and chinkara are in real trouble. Their bodies are light so usually they can leap clear of danger and speed away, but their dainty legs and miniature hooves stick in muddy ground. The more the feral dogs eat, the fitter they become, so eating chinkara fuels them to hunt and eat more chinkara.

Pile up dangers like that and it's tempting for a Bishnoi to quit the desert: who wants to hang around when the land is strewn with the maimed and slain bodies of the wildlife you love? Does having a belief system that tells you to take care of all living beings help you? Or does it pile on the pressure, and add to despair when so much around you is suffering?

That was the choice facing Pooja Bishnoi: despair or act.

Pooja found a maimed chinkara, a female. Instinct took hold. She took her in, cared for her, saved her life. Do it once and you can do it again. Pooja's family owned a patch of land across the road from their house. Walls went up around it, and fences divided the sandy ground inside.

The village is Sribalaji. It is not in a Bishnoi area, but a grouping of thirty-five villages, across six hundred square miles of land, now keep a look-out for injured animals and take them to Pooja's rescue centre. In the last three years she has cared for six hundred and fifty injured animals. The record, so far, for the number of animals brought to her on a single day is fourteen.

Monsoon rains have made the ground muddy and chinkara are doing their best to flee dog packs. Pooja has done some of the dirty work for the day, calming injured chinkara and holding them down on a concrete platform while she administers first aid. The trauma of being rescued always adds to the injuries, as does the loss of blood from their wounds when they struggle to be free from rescuers' hands. After giving first aid, Pooja carries them through the sandy compound to a caged area, where she lays them down to recover. Now Pooja has cleaned up, her shoulder-length hair black and curly. She is wearing a maroon long-sleeve top, the slogan 'Hello Butterfly' above its butterfly image, and Benetton grey trousers with matching trainers.

The notion is to return these chinkara to the wild. It needs to be done within four weeks, before the chinkara become habituated to humans. Out in the wild, if they come too readily to humans they will be prey to dog attacks. Several dozen chinkaras are collected here, and a couple of female nilgai antelopes. When Pooja places a bowl of food on the ground, piles of sweet-scented groundnut leaves and the muskier fodder of dried pods from a khejri tree mixed in with some brittle chickpeas, the animals gather round and heads dip in. The two nilgai reach over the others and baby chinkara nudge between the animal hooves. Some of these babies were brought here as orphans but others were born here – and more, I suspect, are on the way, for in all the excitement a male mounts a female and thrusts into her before scampering off.

That first injured chinkara to arrive is still here, named Sona, meaning beautiful. And she is beautiful, the thick lashes above her vast dark eyes compelling, her legs so thin, and her black thin-toed hoofs as perfect as Cinderella's glass slippers. She has had two babies who will stay here with her. 'Sona does not want to leave,' Pooja says, sneaking her a handful of crushed biscuits.

The two young female nilgai are already twice as large as the chinkara. Now they are fed, they come to the fence, their heads reaching over. The white insides of their ears are marked at their edges by two black flashes, a detail mirrored by the black and white bands on their feet.

On my visit to the Bishnoi in 2020, I visited one of the first protected reserves near the town of Lohawat, open country filled with chinkara. Two years later I have returned. That open land had previously held no animals. But at the local priest's suggestion, the community had raised funds and a vast area of land had been surrounded by walls and high fencing. Soon this fenced reserve would open its gates and chinkara from the town's rescue centre would be brought here. Reality has bitten, an acceptance that new dangers are overwhelming the animals in the wild. Forest officers will collect recovered animals from Pooja's sanctuary but more and more will stay.

Pooja is already on 24/7 alert: how will she manage when she completes her training and finds a job as a teacher? The question seems simple-minded, like asking a young mother if she will abandon her children now she has found herself a job. 'I will manage,' she says.

The provision of animal shelters has been alive in India for thousands of years, with special care taken of cows. The tradition is especially strong in Rajasthan and the states that border it, practised by the Jain community even before Bishnoism came into existence. Pooja is slotting her animal activism naturally into this broad cultural tradition, and it's also worth highlighting a particularly strong Bishnoi factor that has influenced her work: since she was an infant, she has been watching her family, listening to their stories, observing how natural it is to take care of nature.

In a moment we'll meet Pooja's father and brother, but first, here's another example of a Bishnoi learning from their family. For his work in setting up a community-run animal shelter, Peera Ram Bishnoi won the 2018 Royal Bank of Scotland's Earth Hero Award for Animal Conservation; he achieved this while running a small puncture repair shop. He had grown up in a village where his family had a smallholding. They were poor. And yet when he looked out over their field he saw that rabbits, chinkara, deer, peacocks, all manner of wildlife felt free to eat the village crops. 'Why do we let them do that?' the young boy asked. 'Why don't we drive them away?'

'It isn't the wildlife that causes damage to humans,' his father, a subsistence farmer, replied. 'It is the other way around. The existence of the entire universe is dependent upon the *Pancha Maha-Bhoota* (five great elements): earth, sky, wind, fire and water. And every living being that co-exists with us has to be protected. If they dwindle into extinction, how will humans survive?'[44]

Peera Ram took two of the twenty-nine Bishnoi rules especially to heart: 'Be compassionate to all living beings' and 'Do not cut green trees'. 'These were philosophies that I was not only taught as a Bishnoi child,' he recalls, 'but also encouraged to live.'

It is a similar story with Pooja, whose father and brother join us. The father, Ramratan Bishnoi, ran a printing works for many years. He has also written and published dozens of books in Hindi about different aspects of the Bishnoi and wrote and produced a recent feature film about Amrita Devi and the Khejarli martyrs. Farming the family land, he uses no pesticides or fertilisers. Pesticides kill insects, so with the Bishnoi tenet not to kill, their use is out of the question, and fertilisers disturb the natural balance of organisms in the soil. Yes, he notices his neighbours producing bigger crops, but 'I have no regrets,' he says. 'Money does not matter. Environment matters.'

As a child, Pooja shared her home with injured animals taken in by her father. She and her brother have turned their front garden into a memorial for those who died protecting trees at Khejarli, the number 363 formed of sculpted stones and set among flowering plants. Amrita Devi inspired her. 'I wanted to do something for the environment,' she says, 'so I chose this service.'

After making the decision, it's not something she feels the need to think about. 'Being born into a Bishnoi family, you get those values of protecting animals. Being a Bishnoi, it just arises in us.'

Pooja's brother, Laxman, is studying for a PhD in history, and gives fiery speeches on protecting the environment to youth congresses. He's been looking on his sister with pride. 'The west is only angry. You know Greta?' he asks me. 'Greta Thunberg is only angry. We are doing the real work on the ground.'

Isn't there sometimes a space for anger?

'Anger is never good. Overcome it by working.'

Pooja cares for any animal that is brought to her; mostly chinkara, but also rabbits, bee-eaters, vultures, peacocks, eagles, crows, parrots, pigeons and desert cats. Most wounds are caused by feral dogs. Would she treat a feral dog?

Yes, and she has done. She loves dogs too. She has one at home.

Speaking of home, this centre is Pooja's way of 'maintaining ecological balance'. What does she mean by this? One cause of stress for the animals is habitat loss, humans encroaching on space that has been theirs. 'This is my land and I am giving it to the animals. In this way, I am trying to keep the balance.'

Do the animals give her anything in return?

'Yes,' and she smiles. 'They show me selfless love.'

9

The Guru at the Wedding

FOUR WOMEN RECENTLY SET OUT from the University of New Delhi on a joint mission. They headed north, to the city of Jodhpur, from where they dispersed to Bishnoi villages, temples, conservation centres and private homes to meet and speak with Bishnoi women.

As academics, these women shared a field of study: ecological feminism. They held that the forces that disrupt women's lives are the same ones that disrupt the planet. And to find solutions for the planetary crisis they looked for spots in the natural world where women maintain traditional ways of living.

Their research appears to have been open-minded, for while their resultant paper would blame 'patriarchal control' for women's disempowerment and consequent ecological damage, it began with praise of a man.

Guru Jambhoji.

Jambhoji 'strongly opposed the old rudimentary ways of living,' they wrote, 'which were very unkind toward women.'[45] Two of the twenty-nine Bishnoi rules are specific to women: they must be given a break from work when menstruating, and given an uninterrupted month alone with their baby after giving birth.[46]

Jambhoji's first follower, the first Bishnoi, was his uncle, but women soon flocked to him. A majority of these early followers were from the Jat caste, agrarian workers who were seen as outsiders in the traditional temple cultures of India. They did not need temples, Jambhoji assured them. They should not make images of gods, they should simply offer silent chants in praise of Vishnu while they worked their fields. 'The unattainable god will be obtained only by humble people,' he preached.

One of his women devotees was Uma. Jambhoji held her as close as he might a sister, and once gave her a shawl of seven colours from which she derived a new name: Norangi (seven colours). 'She was very devout,' someone from her home village of Rotu told me. 'Every week she made the journey to be with Jambhoji.' 'But he lived sixty miles away,' I counter, 'and back then, by bullock cart, it would have taken a week just to travel there and back, wouldn't it?' A little shake of the head. 'Well maybe not every week. But as often as she could.'

These stories survive and reshape themselves in the telling. And the biggest story was not about the journeys Norangi made to be with Jambhoji, but the one he made to be with her. It's 1515 and Norangi's daughter is to be married. Normally the wife's brother, the girl's uncle, would sponsor the wedding feast by bringing gifts for all the villagers – but Norangi has no such brother. Just her guru.

Now in his sixties, Jambhoji walked down from his hilltop home and climbed onto a bullock cart. Four other holy men rode with him. As wedding gifts, he is bringing blankets for the villagers, and the cart's wooden wheels start rolling along the dirt roads, all on their way to the wedding in Rotu, and followers settle in behind it. While Jambhoji rides in a simple cart, some of these followers travel in carriages, pulled not by oxen but by horses, camels and even by elephants, for within what becomes a procession are sixteen kings and six sultans complete with their retinues. While Jambhoji wears 'clothes of poverty' these nobles wear their finery. That's fine by the guru. 'I am a detached yogi,' he has said, 'and cannot be deluded by worldly desires and illusions. I accept anybody coming to me in any form. I like those who are truthful.'

(A section of Jambhoji's cart remains, bearing an impression of his foot. The foot that alighted on the ground at Rotu also left a deep impression, preserved in the village temple.)

The oxen from the cart were unharnessed from Jambhoji's cart and tethered to a heavy, dead tree. Night fell, and in the morning the oxen were seen to be no longer tethered to a dead old tree, but standing in shade cast by the wide, high crown of a flourishing khejri tree. Blankets as gifts were well and good, the villagers told Norangi, but look! Your guru has turned a stump into a tree! Our land is hot, we have no trees to protect us, so that is the wedding gift we truly need: khejri trees and their shade.

That night, Jambhoji went to work. By the following morning, the fields around Rotu were filled with three thousand seven hundred new khejri trees, already casting deep shade. Those trees would shelter Rotu's villagers for centuries, but on this first morning the villagers had their complaints. 'These trees will attract birds,' they said. 'And not just a few birds. Whole flocks. And those birds will eat the seed we sow on the ground. You have given us trees, but now we will have no crops.'

Jambhoji, of course, had a simple response. Help nature to flourish, and you will flourish too. 'Feed the birds,' he told them. 'Give them the seed you want them to have, and they will not take the seed you need to grow into your crops.'

And so they did, and so it happened.

Mohanlal Bishnoi wears the white costume of Bishnoi men, yet his multicoloured turban of dominant red shows that he's a big noise in the Rotu community. He worked for Rajasthan's civil service but has retired to his village roots. A transparent sticker on his jeep's rear screen packs in the Bishnoi wisdom of life. 'Follow 29 Tenets!' 'Get healthy, wealthy and long life!' 'Be Kind to Living Beings!' 'Do not cut Green Trees!' 'Always Save the Flora and Fauna!'

'All over the world men die for a woman or for money,' Mohanlal declares from the front seat. 'There's only one community that dies for animals and trees.' And we pass out through the other end of the village to acres of land that for centuries the Bishnoi have left undeveloped as wildlife and animal pasture. Such areas are known as *orans*, a term commonly translated as sacred grove, but in fact they are areas of uncultivated grasses and trees. They are maintained for generations in many Indian villages.

Wildlife is common in those villages linked to Bishnoi communities, whose people dig ponds to allow animals to drink, and water is drawn from wells and poured into troughs when the ponds run dry. In Rotu the government has classified this *oran* as an official nature reserve, giving the place extra legal protection.

Mohanlal leads the way onto the land, arms held out like a magician revealing a wonder. And indeed it is beautiful, a spread of perhaps twenty hectares in full view, the land turned into green pasture with the early monsoon rains. Khejri trees, some young and some clearly ancient, grow in planted clusters and as single specimens, a wide sweep of this grassland around them. A herd of blackbuck faces us, then grow wary and run to one side before they settle to graze once again. And flocks of chinkara check us out, reckon we are at a safe distance, and graze on.

Around 85 per cent of the global population of chinkara live in Rajasthan, most of them in the south-west of the state where the Bishnoi concentrate. They flock to any waterhole but can also find enough moisture from plants and dew to survive days without drinking. The Bishnois' love of chinkara is profound. Someone will later show me a phone clip of a Bishnoi woman, smiling at the camera, her bright cotton robe pulled back to bare her left breast at which an orphaned chinkara is suckling.

We move from intense heat to the deep shelter of an old khejri. To the right, in the shade of another khejri, sit two white dogs. 'Don't they chase the animals?' I ask.

'Never,' Mohanlal replies, and then: 'Why aren't you taking notes?'

Fair question. I've become a bit blasé. These aren't my first blackbucks and nor are they the largest herd I have seen. As well as the blackbucks and chinkara on this grassy land, there are cattle, which outnumber them. I'm alert to the small white houses that seem to be encroaching on the space, and the threat of dogs. Mohanlal is telling me stories I already know, including the tale of Jambhoji's miraculous planting of khejri trees. And I have my own interpretation of that story: that Jambhoji gifted the three thousand seven hundred trees, but maybe the servants of the accompanying kings and sultans helped him plant them as saplings and they grew over time. Only later did this tale become the myth of the over-night miracle.

'How big were the trees the morning after Jambhoji planted them?' I ask.

'Big enough for elephants to stand under!' Mohanlal tells me. When I note that down, he smiles.

'Villagers worried that with all these trees, birds would come and steal the seeds for their crops,' Mohanlal continues. 'Jambhoji told them not to worry. The birds would leave here and fly to other fields.'

I raise an eyebrow. This isn't the story as I have heard it.

Mohanlal frowns. He has heard my version of the story but doesn't prefer it. 'Still, the community does spread eighty-five kilos of birdseed each day. Later I will show you. Let's look at the trees.'

As we hurry between blasts of sun, the shade of these khejris is welcome. These are ancient specimens with trunks some twelve feet around, the occasional one hollow at its centre. How did they survive the wildlife who browse the leaves from their sapling shoots? The answer is the phenomenon of self-fencing. A khejri tree starts off its above-ground life by growing horizontal in all directions, becoming a flat and circular bush of thorny twigs. While one central leading shoot spikes higher, animals feed from the mass of peripheral branches and so leave it alone.

A popular dish of the area is *ker sangri*, a fusion of the pods of the khejri with berries from the kheer shrub. Khejri pods start green, and then mature to a chocolate brown, each pod up to eight inches long. Its seeds are held in a dry, yellow, pulp. These pods are known as 'desert beans': soak them for a few hours and then dry them and they are long-lasting. These beans form one part of *ker sangri*, in which the kheer pods are cooked alongside the caper-like berries of the kheer, spiced with carom seeds and red chillies and perhaps stewed in yoghurt. Tree and shrub, khejri and kheer, often grow alongside each other and that is the case here, for beside the ancient khejri is a kheer, a dense tangle of light green stems with their thick green berries.

Large patches of Indian nightshade grow among the thick blades of grass, purple flowers with bright yellow stamens. There are also bleached skulls and vertebrae from animal skeletons, a reminder that this desert, now verdant in the monsoon season, can be harsh. And perhaps, that the feral dogs that are sheltering in the shade of the trees can't fully be trusted.

The day wanes. Trumpets blast inside Rotu's temple. In the village square, a dog howls in response. Drumbeats herald more blasts of the trumpet, and more howls.

Men gather on the temple's marble forecourt. Some smile at the dialogue between trumpet and dog, but they are here in earnest. The sun is setting, pigeons are flocking in to line the temple's sandstone turrets, and the *havan*, the sacred Bishnoi ceremony of fire, begins.

The fire comes from burning dry khejri wood: ghee is poured on as fuel, along with coconut fragments as an offering, and sometimes *bdellium*, a type of gum resin akin to myrrh that adds the fragrance of burnt incense. This fire is seen as purifying the surrounding air.

Men in white turbans and robes sit on rugs spread on the marble terrace, surrounding the priest who tends the fire, chanting from the *shabads*, the written record of Jambhoji's teachings. In all, there are a hundred and twenty *shabads*, taken from different stages in Jambhoji's life of wandering and teaching. 'A wise person is delighted listening to my preaching,' Jambhoji said of this time, 'but an ignorant one gets irritated.' Some men, including Mohanlal, hold the words in their memory, while others use books or smartphone apps.

I'm told these teachings can confound today's young, their meaning locked away inside the text's medieval origins, as distant to them as Chaucer is to native English speakers, and so they chant along without really understanding. I'm reminded of an Islamic scholar, who once explained to me how translating the Koran from Arabic was like translating Mozart; that is to say, it is impossible. The words carry the power of music, and of the moment of their divine delivery. The *shabads* of Jambhoji were composed in fifteenth- and sixteenth-century Marwari, the Hindi dialect spoken in the region, and this verse is chanted in a regular, hypnotic rhythm.

Two girls join the men for a moment, and a woman appears to add ghee to the flames and then leaves. The ceremony is open to women, the men say, but come dusk they are too busy preparing meals or with other tasks.

The trumpets draw closer and the dog wails louder. A procession emerges through the temple doors. A man is holding a large item draped in cloth. It is one of the temple's true treasures, brought out for this ceremony at Mohanlal's request. One such treasure showcased in the temple's shrine is a small rock, set upon a black cushion, which bears that footprint of Jambhoji when he stepped from his cart and onto the ground at Rotu. The other treasure has been locked away. It is the stick of the kheer shrub given by Jambhoji to Prince Rao Duda that he was to wield like a sword.

The procession walks this treasure to the priest, the drape is removed, and the *sword* is revealed. It is not the stick I was expecting but has a scabbard and a long steel blade. I had interpreted the story to mean that Jambhoji's gift of a stick imbued the prince with such confidence he could wield the stick as though it were a sword, and thereby reclaim his kingdom. But here the story is seen as a miracle, with the guru turning a wooden stick into a steel blade so the prince could go armed into a fight.

The blade is held above the flame, to add extra purity to the fire's cleansing powers, and then wrapped back in its cloth and returned to its locked cupboard. The ceremony is at a close.

Jambhoji was sometimes enraged by men exhibiting occult powers, and one such instance happened in Rotu. At the top of a dune at the edge of a village is a shrine to Jambhoji, but another man, Seneya, once held spiritual sway up here. He used his displays of supernatural powers such as levitation to magnetise villagers away from the new Bishnoi path. Told of this rival, Jambhoji climbed the dune and joined Seneya's morning audience.

'What should one do first in the morning,' he asked, 'wash oneself, or eat?'

'Eat,' declared Seneya.

Wrong answer! Jambhoji grabbed Seneya by the hair and dragged him from the hilltop, and then hauled him into the heart of the village, where this occult pretender at last saw sense. Seneya bowed to Jambhoji and was duly initiated into the Bishnoi path.

The route they took is marked today by an iron archway on the edge of the dune's summit, from where a deep groove in the sand runs down to the base. Stand there and look around and you can tell what fields belong to Bishnois, and which to neighbouring villages. The Bishnoi khejris are flourishing. The trees of the neighbours have been woefully cropped and those trees are sick.

Science has recently caught up with Jambhoji's simple fifteenth-century rule: don't cut green trees. In 1999 the Arid Forest Research Institute reported that almost 70 per cent of the khejri trees of some areas of Rajasthan had suffered attacks by a shoot borer (*Derolus discicollis*), a 1.5-inch-long yellowish-brown beetle. It turned out that the severe lopping of the khejris allows the beetles to lay their eggs deep into the tree, with the larvae then eating the sap and heartwood.

Fungal disease then follows. Without treatment, without being spared further lopping, the trees die.

Nights in Rotu are not always peaceful. Peacocks fly up to treetops from where they shriek at each other. Thunder cracks and monsoon rains crash onto roofs and make the black humped bullocks bellow like hippos.

The next morning, as children walk to school and men and women walk to the fields along roads churned to mud, Mohanlal leads us in search of the village goatherd. The goatpen is empty so we make circuits of the village till we find him, his flock of goats nibbling at bushes.

Each goat is male. Normally male kids would be killed once weaned but the community follows the rule not to kill any animal. Each household donates an annual goat levy of two hundred rupees to pay for goat fodder, and billy goats born into neighbouring villages are brought here too when they are weaned.

The village's dairy farm tells its own alternative story of animal husbandry. The sacredness of the cow in Hindu culture means that many Indian villages maintain cow shelters, essentially retirement homes for ageing cattle. This farm is different. Newborn calves are kept inside sheds while out in a large paddock young cows mix with lively bulls and so the herd, started five years ago with thirty cattle, keeps growing. The herdsman works for the love of cows, he says. Khejri trees pool shade on the bare desert earth while the cattle stand in the full morning sunshine, hooded crows on their heads and shoulders.

How can Bishnois, vegetarian but not vegan, drink milk without calves being killed? One teat is always kept for the calf, I am told. Here, there's no thought of running the dairy commercially. Some milk is sold, but only after a calf has stopped feeding from its mother. And milk is heated, given to us guests when scalding hot in a metal beaker, sweet and very rich.

Rotu draws pilgrims and so a *sathri* exists to house them on their visits, a two-storey terrace of white cells that edges a walled area that is a mixture of garden and desert. Inside is a small animal rescue enclosure, where three blackbuck shake in fear at being seen. A patch of sandy ground is where birds feed on the 85kg of seed spread daily, peacocks prominent among them. Pilgrims shed their sandals and climb barefoot up the marble steps to a *mandir*, a shrine to Jambhoji.

An ancient khejri tree is a part of the shrine, its branches growing up through holes cut into the marble of this upper terrace. Jambhoji sat and meditated under this very tree. The marble courtyard with its shrine beneath the spreading branches of the ancient tree feels clean and untroubled, a place of grace.

Sit beneath the tree and questioning minds grow still.

Come away and questions return. I have one about the miracle in Rotu's temple, that sword that is supposed to have sprung magically out of a branch plucked from a tree. Jambhoji's recorded words run counter to the notion that he would arm an exiled prince with a sword and tell him to return and claim his kingdom. 'Do not quote Muhammad to support your animal violence,' Jambhoji told a group of

Muslims. 'His thoughts were quite complex and different from yours. His was the sword of knowledge that removed the sins of the people, not the iron sword!'

Did the wooden stick that Jambhoji handed to a wandering prince turn immediately into a sword? I travelled to the holy temple of Mukam to find my answer.

After his death at Lalasar, Jambhoji's body was transported for burial a day's cart journey south to Mukam. One tale is that the rulers of the cities of Nagaur and Bikaner, each followers of Jambhoji, staked their claims on the guru's body. Mukam was the perfect compromise, equidistant between the two kingdoms.

Mukam can be seen from Jambhoji's hilltop retreat of Samrathal Dhora, cow and chinkara refuges on the slopes of ground in between. Twice a year, in March and October, several hundred thousand Bishnois flock to Mukam. Villages own buildings in the surrounding area – known as *dharmasalas* or community halls – to house them. The main purpose, I am told, is to bring the Bishnoi together, to make sure they are keeping to the twenty-nine precepts, and offer them help if not.

A Bishnoi secretariat, the All India Bishnoi Mahasabha, based in a large three-tiered building that flanks the temple forecourt, is staffed by volunteers that run the operation. They also fund temple construction, offer educational scholarships, and run environmental training courses. During the festivals they police the area too. Anyone found selling tobacco used to be beaten up to teach them a lesson. 'Now we are adapting to more lenient times,' they say.

A mighty white dome tops the Mukam temple, beneath which Jambhoji's tomb is held inside a broad and square floor-to-ceiling column of white marble. This tall inner structure contains Jambhoji's shrine: a sarcophagus is draped with a saffron cloth and strung with malas of black and white beads.[47] Jambhoji himself is buried seven feet underground.

Ganpat, his full name Babal Bishnoi, is in his late thirties, slim and dressed in white, and still with the eagerness and enthusiasm of a young student. He has volunteered to be my guide and translator for much of this trip, and has personal links to Mukam. A self-defined 'rationalist', his last visit here was as a boy sitting on his father's shoulders. The Babal family name links him back through his father to the Babal who was a devotee of Jambhoji, and built the very first temple here. The Babals lobbied, unsuccessfully, for that early temple to be retained when this recent one was built.

That forebear, Ganpat tells me, Randheer Babal, was one of five people taken by Jambhoji to visit heaven. They entered a place of wondrous gardens, waterfalls, and gold in such abundance that even horse carts were made of it. Though these followers were told to bring nothing away with them, Randheer brought back a piece of gold. Jambhoji of course knew everything. 'Why did you steal this gold?' he asked. 'I told you not to.'

'But after you are gone we will have no money to feed people and to build a temple. That is why I stole the gold.'

Jambhoji laughed, and allowed that it was good if the gold could do such work for many years to come.

'It's a true story,' Ganpat the Bishnoi firmly insists, his eyes wide open, staring at me intently. 'Everyone believes in this.'

'Do you?'

Ganpat the rationalist, just as firmly: 'No, I don't.'

It's time for me to meet the head priest at this holiest of
Bishnoi sites and have my questions answered. This is the
equivalent of being brought deep inside the Vatican for a
private audience with the Pope.

I expect grandeur. I'm led through a wooden gate and into
a courtyard surrounded by a cloister. The floor is made of
dirt. The surrounds are blackened plaster falling off walls to
reveal bricks and slack mortaring beneath. To the left, a green
cloth has been tied between the cloister's pillars. Behind this
cloth is Ramanand-ji, cross-legged on his cot. Now, in 2022,
seventy-four years old, Ramanand has been Mukam's high
priest since 1985. He's a solid man with thick arms, a balding
crown and grey hair, his eyebrows dark and quizzical, and a
thick moustache dropping down into bearded jowls.

I ask my questions.

'Is Bishnoism a religion?' I've been arguing that it is, I explain.
Founders of religions tend to stem from other religions.
Jesus was crucified as King of the Jews but Christianity is
not seen as a sect of Judaism. The Buddha began life as a
Hindu prince and left his palace to become a Hindu ascetic,
but with its denial of gods Buddhism is clearly distinct from
Hinduism. While Jambhoji preached that people should
chant the name of Vishnu he spoke against the use of godly
images, welcomed people of all religions, decried the caste
system, created distinct rules to live by, made care for nature
the dominant practice, established new rituals including ones
of conversion, and brought in non-Hindu practices such as

burial of the dead. Yet some Bishnois have kept correcting me. It's a sect, they say. It's a community.

'Yes,' says the high priest, 'Bishnoism is a religion. It is not a sect. A sect is a path to a religion. A religion is universal, for the whole world. Hinduism is concerned for people. Bishnoism is concerned for the whole environment.'

Does he feel that concern for the environment is especially acute now, in an era of climate change?

The Bishnoi have been preparing for this for a long time. 'Five hundred and eighty years ago,' the high priest tells me, 'Jambhoji knew what we are learning now.'

Other religions allow women priests. Might the Bishnoi go the same way?

He laughs. 'Women are holy. We see them as the goddess Deva. We give them whatever they want, but they have never asked for this. I have never heard such a thing. They are busy doing what they do.'

Maybe in the future, in fifty years?

'Who knows? I do know, from looking at some Hindu groups, that women pay more attention when the priest is a woman.'

I bring him my concerns about the story of Jambhoji and Rao Duda, when the young guru gave the prince a stick and told him to wield it like a sword. I've seen people worship the sword, I tell him. They believe the stick, as it was passed between the two men, instantly became that sword. Is that the meaning of the story, or is it a myth? I read the story as being one about confidence: carry the stick as you would a sword, have faith in who you are, and you regain your power.

The stick remained a stick, he believes. It did not turn, supernaturally, into a sword. 'The stick gave him confidence!' He does, however, believe in Jambhoji's miracle at Rotu, where the area was transformed overnight with khejri trees big enough to drop shade over resting camels.

As regards Jambhoji's teachings, though, here's what is most important, Ramanand-ji says. Jambhoji taught us in his *shabads* that all his teachings must be taken as a whole. You can't pick and choose.

And I ask him about the young, who in the West at least are increasingly anxious about climate change. Should they be nervous?

'They have lost their way, their *dharma*,' he says. 'They have lost their religion. They should take care of nature. They should take that as their religion.'

Which is exactly the message a man we are about to meet took away from his pilgrimage to Mukam sixty years ago.

10

The Man who Plants Trees

CAN YOU BRING TREES TO THE DESERT, and have them grow? Ranaram Bishnoi hadn't given it much thought. It was 1962. He was twenty-five. He worked with what he was given, which consisted of some fields around the village of Ekalkhori. He farmed them, making the most of monsoon rains to grow crops in the desert. Sand dunes were encroaching to swallow the edges of his fields, but such is desert life.

Being a devout Bishnoi, Ranaram joined one of that year's vast bi-annual gatherings at the temple at Mukam. The authorities had brought in a speaker. Back in the fifteenth century most of Jambhoji's early followers, the first Bishnois, were agrarian workers who came from the Jat caste. Gyan Prakash Bilania was not a Bishnoi, but he was a Jat and had become president of the Jats' ruling council. A police superintendent who held a series of government posts, he had built a reputation as a leader of farm workers and at this 1962 gathering he set out to goad the crowds with a rousing speech.

'Why on earth are you here?' he asked.

The crowd stared at him, speechless.

'It's your religion to plant trees and take care of living organisms. So don't waste your time coming here and feeling good about yourselves. Go home and plant trees!'

In one man at least, the words struck home. Ranaram was a farmer, so planting trees should hold no problems. From the Mukam festival he headed to a tree nursery in Bikaner, where he bought some saplings. Back home, he planted them.

His mission had begun.

Problem one: those saplings from the Bikaner nursery were a real weight when grouped in his hands and he could imagine each growing into a tree: dig a hole, spread the sapling roots, cover them with earth and water them, and you could believe you were planting a forest. Each would grow so tall. Step back, though, and the reality looked bleak, for all Ranaram could see were a few twigs sticking out of acres of sand. And look to one side and all he could see was sand, amassed in the weight of shifting dunes. It would need more than his armload of saplings to keep this sand in place.

He needed more trees.

Problem two: find the trees. In a desert land inhabited by subsistence farmers, his village of Ekalkhori had no use for tree nurseries. Nor was it linked to any transport routes. It took endless turns through narrow country lanes to reach the village, so bus routes didn't include it. And the nearest train station was twelve miles away. The lucky thing? A train from that station went to Jodhpur, where Indian Railways had a plant nursery. So Ranaram walked the twelve miles to the station, took the train, selected his stock, and rode back.

Problem three: it was hard to be confronted by so many trees in the nursery and not buy them. By the time he had collected them together, his bundle of saplings weighed fifty kilograms. No problem! Ranaram was a big and vigorous man. Pile them on the train, step out at the nearest station to home, strap the saplings to his back, and he only had twelve miles to walk to carry them. So he did so.

Again and again. Week after week. Year after year.

Problem four: some saplings didn't take to their surroundings. Was this because Ranaram did not know enough? As a child, because the nearest school was twenty miles away, Ranaram seldom attended it. But he had a natural intelligence. Study nature, and it could teach him what he needed to know.

Which saplings failed to grow? Those with black roots. He had planted those and watched them die. But those with red or brown roots could adapt just fine. And they grew into a whole mix of different trees: the neem, a fast-growing mahogany; rohida, known as 'desert teak', which took surprisingly well to the extreme high and low temperatures of the dunes, and every springtime the magnificent state flower of Rajasthan blazed from its branches, tubular flowers of red, orange and yellow with four stamens reaching far out to pull in neighbourhood insects; a number of fig species, attracting pollinators to their fruits; the desert-adapted khejri and kankeri of course, the two trees most beloved of the Bishnoi; and bougainvillea, a desert shocker with its exuberance of blooms.

And then there was the babool tree, a thorny acacia with waxy leaves like the khejri and known to have medicinal qualities, but while it was drought tolerant it was an invasive species and offered no use to animals or people. Villagers planted it for firewood. Ranaram studied the trees as they grew, and watched the birds. None went to the branches of the babool, none nested there. He noticed how the trees to each side of the babools barely flourished, as though the babools sucked up all the earth's resources for themselves, and struck them off his tree nursery list.

Nature kept giving him lessons, and he kept learning.

Problem five: planting the trees in sand. The monsoons solved that one. Wait for the months of July, August and September, and the rains were enough to hold the sand together. You could dig a fine hole and pack moist sand around it, maybe adding a touch of dung. Add a tube alongside the sapling through which to pour the water so that it reaches the deepest of the roots, and the roots can then keep growing down to where the ground retains moisture.

However, this was a desert, with minimal water. Come the four summer months, from March through June, temperatures reached extreme highs and no rains fell on the sun-baked land. To survive the summer, each tree needed twenty litres of water. Every morning. And the same at close of day. That was forty litres of water per tree, per day. Plant a hundred trees a year, and that was a daily need for four thousand litres of water. And of course a hundred trees, stuck into acres of desert sand, pretty much disappeared, so Ranaram couldn't hold himself back and planted hundreds and hundreds each year. That meant three million litres of water a season. Each litre weighed a kilo. And the nearest water source was a well several miles away. How do you haul millions of litres of water from the well to the trees?

Ranaram rented a camel and a cart. A temple dedicated to the Hindu monkey god Hanuman, pink and palatial with slender towers in the North Indian temple style, its domes pinched and stretched high and curving gently to their points, crowns a small hill at the far edge of the village. Beneath the temple lay the village's well. Ranaram parked his camel cart, wound water up in buckets from the well's depths, poured it to fill the containers on the cart, steered the camel along the four miles of lanes, and then ferried the water by hand up to the saplings, his feet digging into the shifting sand, twenty kilos per tree in the morning and the same in the afternoon. Through a hundred and twenty days of blazing heat, till the monsoons took over the watering and he could go back to planting.

Problem six: how do you pay for the saplings, the train journeys, the hiring of the camel, and find the money to feed and clothe your family, when you are a poor subsistence farmer who dedicates seven months a year to planting trees?

Call that a problem? Ranaram had strength. And he had five months a year when his trees could survive without him. He left his family and hired himself out through those winter months as a plasterer on building sites. The money he earned helped keep his family, and pay for his trees. And he bought in a little help too, recruiting women from the village, paying them two rupees for each tree they planted.

His home lay halfway between the well and the ten-acre desert patch of government land that he was filling with trees. When his younger son, Vishek, was five years old he hoisted the boy on his shoulders and walked him the two miles to the dunes. It was time for the boy to have a meaningful life: Vishek scampered up the sand dune in his father's wake and was shown how to plant his first tree.

'My father dedicated his entire life to planting trees in our village,' Vishek later told a TV station. 'For him, planting trees is not a responsibility or a job, it's part of his daily routine. Just like breathing is important for us, planting and nurturing trees is for him. From him I learned that nature will take care of us, but first we must take care of nature.'

The car windows wind down, the driver asks questions, and a parade of people gleam with sudden understanding, and say 'Ahhu' – 'Tree man' – because that's how the locals know Ranaram. A middle-aged goatherd with gold weighing down the lobes of his ears; eleven-year-old boys in tan shirts on a street corner; mechanics and shop owners and drivers; all direct us forward, till finally an elderly man in the white costume and turban of a Bishnoi climbs into the car and guides us to a fence that edges two stone-block houses. 'There's Ranaram!' and points up to a figure on the ridge of a dune.

Ranaram's son Vishek comes out to greet us, and pulls out a daybed for us to sit on. It's in the shade of a neem tree, just twelve years old but already eighteen foot tall with a thick crown of leaves. The sand beneath it is studded with tiny saplings from where the neem seeds have fallen, for it seems trees can't resist growing here.

'Please, let's first go up and meet Ranaram,' I ask. It is eleven o'clock and he has been out tending his trees since sunrise. 'Careful, careful,' people call as I step on sand cracks up the hillside path and stumble as the ground subsides.

Ranaram stands and waits near the top of the dune path. He has one of those Bishnoi power voices that I have heard called 'a voice of lions' and booms questions above my head. Dressed in a white *dhoti* and singlet, a grey moustache trimmed neatly above his upper lip, a white turban coiled on his head, he is carrying a walking stick and a flat trowel and small scythe. He is a vast man, his chest broad, his arms thick. He is eighty-five years old

He learns why we have come, relaxes, and is soon cracking jokes. 'A woman gives birth to sixteen children and I plant five trees, but that is harder, because after giving birth she no longer loses blood, but I bleed every day.' He points to the latest cuts and scratches on his arms, and we note the broad spots of blood dried across the singlet.

Before he sits cross-legged and accepts our questions, he shows us the view. We are standing on a dune, the panorama is wide, and the view is bucolic. This is desert as transformed by one man's sixty years of planting trees; people tot up that he has planted more than fifty thousand in this area.

Heavy early monsoon rains have helped, casting a green wash over much of the land, but look around and you can understand the concept of a desert forest, for wherever you look you see trees. They line the ridge of the dune where we are standing, shade the houses of the village and grow thick around the Hanuman temple in one direction, and way over to the right is the range of dunes that are now home to most of

Ranaram's planted trees. The trees are all full-crowned, green and healthy, and abundant. They don't crowd each other, but fill the landscape and fulfil the definition of a forest – an eco-system in which trees are the dominant life form.

This was an impossibly wide canvas on which to work, one man against mountains of shifting sand, and shows what one person can do, tree by tree. 'Beautiful,' I say.

Ranaram accepts the English word, he smiles, and we settle down on the ground. His hands sweep gestures as he tells his tales, and he strokes and pats and finger-punches my translator Ganpat's legs and arms to press home his main points of argument. 'Who has more rights on this planet? The plants and the animals. They were here long before we humans. Now we've become powerful, and if we refuse to give them their rights, the very least we can do is hold our greed in check so as not to destroy them.'

His voice stays rich and loud, as though he is used to holding conversations with people standing on distant dunes. While he speaks, birds in the surrounding trees are singing.

'There's no end to our greed,' he adds. 'But without these plants and animals we cannot survive. Thorn bushes won't keep a man from destroying the ecology. Fences won't do it. The only thing that can help is awareness.'

Amrita Devi gave her life for a tree, and that provides Ranaram with one acute example of awareness. 'Your life will end, you will lose it,' he says, 'but a tree will give happiness, life, shelter and food to many generations. You are a single entity, and a tree is for many.'

He tells the story of his life, from hearing the 'go home and plant trees' message when he was twenty-five through the ensuing six decades of total tree dedication. Villagers followed his example, took saplings from him, and trees surround their homes as well. The dunes that he planted are government land. The government noted their transformation, and called him to the city five times, each time to receive a medal, and eventually gave him the award he needed: they drilled two bore holes near their dunes. He can now water them without hiring a camel.

With the money he saved from camel hire, he bought thirty thousand saplings. 'I gave them to the surrounding villages,' he says. 'And have planted trees as far away as Delhi, in the state of Haryana, and in the Punjab. And the government invited me to join a mission to Nepal. I carried a khejri with me, but the Nepalese border guards stopped me. They made me plant it on the Indian side of the border. The Nepalese are lovely people, but they were all very small.

'My father and mother were both huge, but those were different times. Babies were born weighing seven or eight kilos, and now they weigh only two.' He presses his hand around Ganpat's biceps, feeling for strength and not finding much, and laughs. With a fist, he beats his chest. 'My own mass and strength come from being of the agrarian caste, working hard to gain a fine physique. And because I eat good food, and drink cows' milk.'

Ganpat pays close attention, smiles, translates, and gathers bruises from Ranaram's frequent pokes and pinches. 'I am a broken man,' Ranaram roars. 'Vishek's wife, my daughter-in-law, died recently. I long to find a new wife for my son, but it's hard. For every thousand men in Rajasthan there are only nine hundred women. Maybe Vishek has had his share.'

The translation pauses but the conversation continues, as Ranaram asks of any available women in Ganpat's village. And then he goes silent, and we listen to birdsong for a while.

'I love the variety of their nests,' he says, 'each different for each bird, at different heights, some seen and some always hidden. Every morning I spread grain for the birds and the chinkara, and down there,' he points to his field below us, 'I am going to build a platform for bird feeding. I was going to build it high in a tree, but foresters tell me lower is better. It attracts most birds.'

Sometimes he climbs his wooded dunes and sits under one of his trees. 'I have planted this tree,' he says to himself. 'It is giving shade to me, to others, to animals, to birds, and to many in the future.' He is especially pleased at what the trees offer to birds. 'This is a *dharmasala* of birds,' he says. 'No-one disturbs them when they are in the tree.'

Covid saw Ranaram hospitalised, but when friends called to arrange a visit he told them not to bother. He'd be checked out from his hospital bed before they got there. His trees needed him.

Does he ever wake in the morning and think, well maybe not today? Let's give myself a break?

'Never. Not at all. I never even think of it. I have taken this work to its climax, but I am still strong.'

He rises to his feet; it's an effort, he grunts with the pain of it, then off we stride, back down the dune path to the cot beds in the shade of the neem tree. Ranaram only plants neem and khejri trees now, but has grown kankeri saplings from seed. He distributes them to people for planting.

'You must take one back to your village,' he tells Ganpat, and walks off to fetch one.

His wife brings us clay beakers of tea, and Vishek brings out his phone. 'A film about my father played on French TV,' he says, 'and then there is this.' He shows us Ranaram's picture on the cover of *India Today*.

Vishek is proud. Yet there's still place for some father-son rivalry. 'What my father has done is great, but it is nothing compared to the sacrifice of Amrita Devi. Now climate change is hitting the whole world, we have the same temperatures in Rajasthan, Europe, even New York, and only one community have given their lives to stop this: those three hundred and sixty-three people who died at Khejarli three hundred years ago. The world must know their story and learn from their model.'

Vishek has formed an NGO, Global Green Mission 363, with the intent of gaining global recognition for the martyrs of Khejarli. The world needs to learn from their sacrifice. Their story should be included in India's school syllabus, and the site of the massacre should be declared a Unesco World Heritage Site.

Ranaram returns, the kankeri sapling in his hand. The sapling is six inches high, inside its handful of earth. Using strips of white cloth, he turns it till it is securely bound, in a custom-made white cloth pot. 'For your village,' he says, and hands it over to Ganpat. 'You must ask a girl to plant it.'

And so we do.

11

How to Make a Tree Planter

GANPAT'S VILLAGE OF PHITKASNI is sixteen miles from Jodhpur, though the city is fast encroaching. His house is newly built, on the roadside edge of a ten-acre field where full-crowned khejris stand among the lines of millet. Ganpat's tried planting new trees, but can't fence in his whole land so camels and nilgai chomp down the tender saplings. To give Ranaram's kankeri a chance, Ganpat has his young son dig a hole close to the protection of the house.

It's a Sunday morning, peacocks shrill from the tops of khejris, and guests arrive for the ceremony. Ganpat's teenage niece is designated chief tree planter. She unwraps its white cloth banding and nestles the sapling into its hole, holding it in place while others shovel in soil. The tree is watered, photos are taken, and guests look for new, related entertainment.

A trip to the far side of the village fits perfectly. Ranaram had recruited women to help in his tree planting, and then asked for a girl to plant the tree he gave to Ganpat. In the village of Phitkasni, five hundred local women have recently planted two trees each. Rao Ridmil, a young man sturdy in his T-shirt with a soft beard on his face, leads a short expedition to see them.

'My mother is the village *serpench*,' he says. A recent government decree requires half of the country's *serpenches*, the elected village leaders, to be female. Rao's mother, Shanti Devi, was elected. Mother and son consult, but she leaves him to do the work. The village's waste water used to spread over the land of scrub and fields we pass through. Now it is gathered in three new filtration ponds, each rimmed by low walls of red clay that are decorated with white floral motifs. 'This scheme is funded by a government initiative,' Rao explains as he walks us around, 'but this is one of only ten villages in Rajasthan to have taken it up.'

We take time to admire the water collected in the third pond, coloured green but now clean enough to be carried back to the land. 'It's good enough for watering,' Rao says. 'We persuaded five hundred women from the village each to plant two trees. And not just plant them, but to pledge to keep their two trees alive. Five hundred women and a thousand trees. The trees bond them. They come to the pond and collect the filtered water, and take this to the trees they have fostered.'

And we visit the trees. Some are around the perimeter of these ponds, planted into holes a foot deep and wide.

As we drive back to Ganpat's farm the new trees become obvious, planted around the village's small Bishnoi temple and all along the lanes.

Back at the house, awaiting lunch, I meet another of the tree-planting guests. Anil Bishnoi, a slim man in his late forties with a lean face and close-cropped greying hair, is originally from this village of Phitkasni but now lives in Jodhpur with his wife and two children, where he works as a doctor. He sits beside me and speaks of his philosophy.

'A person can survive ten days without food, and three days without water. Indian fasts give us evidence of this,' he begins. 'And a person can last just one minute without oxygen. What gives us oxygen?'

I have learned the correct answer to this. Time and again Bishnois have told me how trees give us oxygen.

'Trees,' I say.

'Of course. Ask any man whether he has cut down a tree, and the answer is likely yes. Ask him if he has planted a tree, and the answer is likely no.'

The Vedas, he tells me, the collection of Hindu's most celebrated scriptures, composed in Sanskrit around five thousand years ago and passed down through generations, are no longer read. 'The young now have their phones, they stream Netflix, and in truth when did I last consult the Vedas myself? The present education system has ruined us. Previously education was practical, and students gained skills. Now it's theoretical, and the skills that are gained are zero.'

Anil has an MD in forensic medicine and toxicology, works at a medical college that is linked to three hospitals, and on top of that 'day job' he runs his own private hospital. This is clearly enough work for any man. And these are good jobs, caring for people. You could excuse a man for doing no more with his life, using his free time for gentle society in which to express opinions. But this man is a Bishnoi. The notion that 'I would like to do more, of course I would, but my life is too busy' seems alien to Bishnois. Thinking prompts action.

And so Anil also founded and runs the National Medicos Organisation (NMO) Green Drive. Their motto: 'Don't make trees rare; keep them with care.'

On 26 January 2022 – Independence Day – the National Medicos ran a series of programmes. Five hundred doctors formed medical teams and stationed themselves in one hundred and twenty-one slum areas around the country. They took people's blood pressure, administered basic nutritional tests and, when these showed a person was needy, they provided the food ingredients for a nutritional boost. They also sanitised people's hands and demonstrated how to keep nails clean, since such hygiene was lacking. Indian flags were raised on slim poles. And then Anil added a 'green drive' element to the venture: in a hundred and one of the villages they selected a child and together planted a tree, which they asked the child to adopt.

To help the child keep the tree alive, the medicos taught a technique of slow watering: a terracotta pot is placed, tilted and part buried in the hole beside the sapling. The pot has a hole in its side and is filled with sand. 'The children and the trees will grow together, till the tree is bigger than the child who can then stand in its shade. Every Independence Day we'll go back, and the team of doctors will check on each tree and its child custodian. These children have little else to call their own, but now they have a tree they can care for.'

Those hundred and one trees, it gradually becomes clear, are a happy by-product of the Green Drive's work, but not the purpose. Their focus isn't on creating forests; it's on turning people into tree planters.

India has six hundred and thirty medical colleges, each one host to a Green Drive unit. 'Lecturers invite new medical students to plant a tree,' Anil tells me, 'and then keep it alive for the five years of their training. Senior teachers and doctors plant and adopt trees too. Seeing the habit in those they respect develops the practice in others. I took my eight-year-old and three-year-old with me to water my trees. Seeing this, students joined in.'

Each college has roughly a thousand students, and out of these a hundred take the pledge to plant and nurture a tree. Or maybe a plant. Students are given an indoor plant, ones that give out oxygen twenty-four hours a day, and they promise to keep that alive. Anil shows me the project's Facebook page. Post after post shows a young student posed beside their plant or tree, sometimes with a group of friends gathered to admire the act of planting. These students post their picture, with their plant or with a tree going into its hole in the earth. 'They add their details,' Anil explains, 'the type of tree or plant and where it is located. The tree is tagged with the matching information. In that way, anyone noticing that a tree is ailing can send an alert to its carer.'

First thing each morning, Anil posts a cheery message into the Green Drive project's WhatsApp group, spurring the students on. Medical students who take part each receive a certificate. The Green Drive has a citizen's wing as well, made up of patients and their families. 'They need more than certificates,' Anil says. 'For the citizens' project we offer what we call "temptations". They show us proof of successful tree planting, and then maybe in return we speed up waiting lists, or offer a twenty per cent discount on procedures.'

The project started in 2017, with two thousand trees planted in the early days. Anil's college is attached to four hospitals whose bare grounds are becoming forest. The hospital's managers offered no support, but nor did they object. 'Why would they? We were taking care of their empty land. Transforming it. People should take care of animals too. It would do them so much good. Write about that. Tell people to take an animal into their home and look after it. Or if they are in a city, maybe they can group together and support a herdsman and a cow and share the milk.'

Anil now lives in the city. What's that like?

'We live in a modest, square house. There is noise twenty-four hours a day and nowhere to take a walk. That was my inspiration to start the Green Drive project. People don't read the Vedas, but they can see good practice and therefore emulate it. They see lecturers, doctors, students, patients, anyone planting a tree, and then caring for it, they notice this. They see what a difference planting a tree can make.'

'And then maybe they become tree planters?'

'That's right. It doesn't matter whether people plant one tree or a thousand trees. One tree or a thousand trees equals one unit. It is not about the number of trees planted, but the number of individuals engaged in the act of planting a tree and nurturing it. Care for a tree, and you come to appreciate how much it is giving you in return.'

Perhaps it's part of his being a doctor, for while Anil speaks of 'the huge power of people', he sees that they need healing.

'We've become unhinged from the natural world,' he says. 'Jambhoji saw how this had happened during his fifteenth-century drought, and gave people rules to reconnect them with nature. Loss of direct connection with the natural world diminishes people. Adopt and nurture a tree, and you are reconnected. It's the way of life for the Bishnoi, but everyone can do it. People are dynamite. Dynamite without ignition. The Bishnoi can ignite the dynamite. When humans and nature reconnect in a deep way, everything is possible.'

12

Women in the City

WE'RE BACK IN THE CITY, where dogs slink between traffic and along street walls. There's no room for them in the city's dog pounds: these are so overfilled that strays are trucked out to the countryside. Bishnoi villagers feed them bread, because they're soft-hearted where animals are concerned and they also hope that staving off the dogs' hunger will prevent them chasing down chinkara for their food.

It is permitted to sterilise these dogs. In October 2023, in league with the charity Humane Society International, Bhutan became the first country in the world to neuter and vaccinate all its 150,000 street dogs, but India is yet to grapple with the problem. I don't bring it up with Devangini because she is fierce in her love for animals and I suspect she would give the idea of a mass sterilisation programme short shrift. Sparky and alert with waves of black hair and a bright yellow dress, twenty-something Devangini is entirely a city creature of the twenty-first century.

'It's a choice,' she says of her clothing. 'A woman can wear the veil or not. For some, the veil is comfortable. If someone wants to marry outside of their caste, it can be done. Krishna said that religion must adapt to the times, and in this era everything is changing. What must be done is to learn from the ways of the elders; you can't just go it alone.'

She lives with her parents in their family home in Jodhpur. Some puppies were outside in the yard. 'Did you see them?' Devangini asks. She has a passion for dogs, for animals, perhaps for everything. 'There were six at first. The mother ran away so I nursed them. The woman neighbour complained. You should kill them, she said. Put this poison in their milk and have them drink it. Her husband was a wing commander who hunted chinkara on air force land. The couple had their own German shepherd, locked safe in the house.

'"You say you love your dog?" I told them. "That's not love; it's selective love. You must show compassion."

'The wing commander got in his car and deliberately ran over one of the puppies and killed it. I went round to protest. How could anyone kill a dog? The action was caught on a neighbour's CCTV camera. The Bishnoi Tiger Force said they would come round and protest outside the wing commander's house, but I said no, we'll handle this by using the law. I sent the evidence of the killing to the police and posted the film clip on social media. It immediately got a thousand likes.

'The puppies were terrified by the incident. They lived on the street with cars passing close by all the time and now barked at every one. All the neighbours complained. "You must get rid of those dogs," they said.

'"The only difference between these dogs and yours is that they are homeless," I told them. "You give them their own home and they'll be alright."

'The puppies got sick. They were too many to carry in my arms so I took them in a taxi to the vets. "These puppies have parvovirus," the vet said. "There is almost no chance of saving them."

'"Then take that chance," I said. "Whatever it costs." The puppies were saved.'

When the weather is hot the family leaves their gates open so the dogs can come in and find shade. They have two house dogs: one a perky black Indian former street dog with large pert ears named Jackie, allowed into the house to become a much loved pet, the other a lugubrious German shepherd. Between these house pets and the five street dogs who come and go from the compound, dogs consume a half of the family's outlay on food.

Though she is living in the centre of Jodhpur, Devangini takes whatever chance she can find to connect with the natural world. 'I found a sparrow fallen from the nest, still without its feathers. I went online to find out how to feed a sparrow chick and did my best. I kept it alive for three months, but it can't have had the nutrition its mother would have given it and died. My whole family was heartbroken, weeping as though we had lost a child.'

Vijay Laxmi Bishnoi is related to Devangini's family and has driven up from Jaipur to join our conversation. Her father,

Poonam Chand Vishnoi, spent five years in the 1980s as Speaker of Rajasthan's State Legislature (to set that in a global context, Rajasthan has a population larger than France or the United Kingdom's). A photograph of father and daughter hangs in the entrance hall of the Bishnoi Mahasabha head-quarters in Mukam. Vijay Laxmi Bishnoi followed her father into politics, became Rajasthan's Minister for Arts, Culture and Tourism, and once led the Women's Wing of the Indian National Congress Party.

She is fluorescent in a saree of deep-pink-patterned gold, her hair a tumble of rich black curls, with eyes that sparkle, engage, and appraise. 'There are no steps to becoming a Bishnoi,' Vijay Laxmi tells us. 'You can only be one.'

And then she recounts a powerful story: 'When my grandmother was six or seven years old she was playing with peafowl eggs and broke five of them. She didn't know better. And she regretted it later. When she got mar-ried, she lost five children in a row. She believed that was because she took those eggs. "It left me to feel how the peahen felt," she said. Her sixth child was born healthy and stayed alive.'

Talented at school, Vijay Laxmi wished to follow a scientific career, but her father knew of two Bishnoi women who had become doctors and then married out of caste. He saw science as being causal to that lapse in tradition, and so Vijay Laxmi was consigned to the arts. She was engaged at fifteen, and married after graduation.

Which brings us to the subject of marriage and caste. Arranged marriages are a pan-Indian concept also adopted by the Bishnoi, though Jambhoji's teachings don't recommend them. The Bishnoi commentator Inder Pal Bishnoi argues that Jambhoji 'never preached discrimination, untouchability, caste-creed, inferior-superior and high-low on the basis of birth'.[48] And in *Shabad 39*, Jambhoji points out: 'Everyone has the same breath, the same flesh and the same life force in their body. Then why should you consider anyone to be inferior or superior. Oh people, why do you discriminate against others?'

Devangini sparks back into life. 'It's agreed that I don't need to marry before I have settled into my profession,' she says. 'And I think that is right. Also ...'

Her father interrupts. 'It is the number one rule in our society that nobody marries inter-caste,' he calls out, and the speech freezes on Devangini's lips.

Vijay Laxmi reclaims the conversation. 'You may well hear it from others, so it's better you hear it from me.'

She takes a short breath, and the next sentence comes out with the cadence of a sigh. 'My own son married inter-caste.'

For me, of course, this is no more shameful than the statement 'my son married for love', though within Bishnoi society it is an aberration. Such an act can cast not only the child but also the child's parents out of Bishnoi society. It has clearly been bruising for Vijay Laxmi, though when a male (unlike a female) marries out of caste their child can still be a Bishnoi. Vijay Laxmi has hopes pinned on her young Bishnoi grandson.

What lesson should the rest of the world pick up from the Bishnoi?

Devangini's heart is still going out to animals. 'No life form wants to die. Slaughter in any form must be banned. If you can't take care of them, at least don't make their life more miserable.'

'People should turn to vegetarianism,' Vijay Laxmi says. 'And this is not just to spare animals from slaughter. There is *sattvic* food, which imparts clean, good vibes to those who eat it. Such is vegetarian food. And then there is *tamasic* food, which saps energy from the body. We are what we eat, and food brings to a human spiritual as well as physical qualities.'*[49]

She calls, too, for people to look at the examples of Bishnoi women. 'Our women take in orphan fawns and breastfeed them even before feeding their own child. I have even seen women breastfeeding orphaned baby monkeys. What other women do this? You should find a good Bishnoi woman and marry her.'

'But then you would have to cast both of us out.'

Vijay Laxmi laughs. 'Yes, that is true.'

Devangini's house is being renovated. Her father leads me to the balcony to look down on the small front yard. Two tall thin trees grow there, inside the shelter of a wall that fronts the street. The basic geometry of the house dictates that the trees should make way so that a new gate can give

* Professor Vinay Kumar Srivastava notes how the Bishnoi would rather eat nothing than vegetarian food cooked in a non-vegetarian kitchen. They are not so concerned about what others eat: 'The emphasis is on the purification of the individual. If the individual is purified he will be in a position to purify others, his or her community.' (See also endnote 41.)

cars easy access to their parking spots. Instead a gate will be placed elsewhere, look misaligned, and vehicular entrances and exits will be awkward. 'But we will still have our trees,' the father says.

Bishnois plant trees and save trees, but what do they do when the trees are gone?

13

The Massacre
of the Trees

THE SKIES ABOVE THE THAR DESERT are filled with visible stars, and with satellites that map the desert floor. A highway runs between the cities of Bikaner and Phalodi, and satellite images capture its stream of traffic. In the miles-wide stretch of desert land beside the road they show the tall steelwork of electricity pylons and the squat grey towers of transmission stations. But in photographs taken the year before they show broad round shapes that are the crowns of mature khejri trees and the shade they pool across the dry land.

Look again. Were those khejri trees – hundreds and hundreds of them spread over a fifteen-thousand-acre parcel of desert – really there? An official form signed and stamped by a local government officer stated that they were not. Stand there now. Look around. See? No trees. Why should this site not have been chosen for the erection of a field of solar panels?

For some weeks, newspaper reports have featured short articles, illustrated by photos of young Bishnois protesting in front of government buildings. Then the protesting crowds, and the articles, grew. The protests were started by one man, Kailash Bishnoi. He's back on site now, a taut guy with dark eyes and hair, a beard that grows into his neck. 'Being Human' is stamped on the chest of his black shirt. Two strands of thick gold chain dip inside his white undershirt. What's this?

'I wear gold,' he says in a voice of quiet thunder, another of the Bishnoi with a 'lion's roar' of a voice. 'It makes my heart strong.'

He pulls the pendant out from his shirt.

'Lion's claws!' And there they are, two lion's claws reaching left and right from a broad ridge of gold.

'My English weak,' Kailash says. 'My love of khejri very strong!'

I ask what he does.

'I work in agriculture. I have a petrol pump. And I do social service. Service for animals and khejri trees.' He has a small farm, fields that are currently growing cotton, a wife and two children and a hundred-and-four-year-old grandmother who is as bright as a button. He is also the *serpench* for his village.

We were to wait for a 'camper' to come and ferry us further across the desert, but Kailash is not a man to wait very long so after thirty seconds we march off. Friends are in tow. He directs my feet toward the compacted sand left by tyre tracks.

'Are you with Bishnoi Tiger Force?'

'No, I am alone. I am with no organisation.'

'Then how can you do things, one man alone?'

He grips an imaginary phone. 'I have many, many friends.'

One of these friends, Bhagirath, is with us. A tall and seem-ingly mild man in his thirties, he farms the neighbouring land, saw what was happening to the khejri trees, and phoned Kailash who sprang into action.

'Is this you following the model of Amrita Devi?' I ask Kailash.

'No! I am not a tree hugger.' He flashes out a fighting pos-ture, one fist behind the other in a punching gesture. He is a fighter. What has happened is that an energy company has stripped this fifteen-thousand-acre parcel of its khejri trees in order to position its arrays of solar panels.

'Did people try and argue with you that the solar panels were green energy?'

'This is green energy!' He shapes a tree with his hands, moulding its trunk then spreading his arms and hands high to show leafing branches. 'A khejri gives oxygen, it gives food, it gives nitrogen. How can you cut it down and say that is green energy?'

It wasn't even necessary to cut down the trees. This isn't a case of either you get clean energy or you keep the trees. You can have both. The energy companies who are building solar plants in Bikaner have found a way of positioning new arrays of solar panels so that they co-exist with the khejris. Here there was no willingness to do that.

Kailash tells of a recent mass protest, in which Bishnois from across the region filled jeeps and trucks and raced to this area of felled trees. 'Old people,' and Kailash pinches in his shoulders and bends forward to mime old age. 'Many old people came. And women. And children.' His hand levels out to show their small sizes. 'Priests from the temple at Jambha. Everybody comes from everywhere. And we were against bodyguards.'

The police accompanied the Bishnoi protestors into the desert of lost trees, which was now officially designated a worksite. This demonstration was legal because it was in accord with Bishnoi religious beliefs. Even so, Kailash was arrested along with others and charged with disrupting the work of the solar plant.

A white SUV comes. Kailash opens the front passenger door. 'Martin, you are guest!' Kailash jumps in to share the single seat and others crowd the back while one man rides shotgun, reaching his phone in through the window to click photos. The jeep bounces and sways over ridges.

We stop. Kailash jumps out. 'Martin, come!'

He shows me to some felled trees.

'Look. Look how big. Look how long!'

And he moves forward and strokes the dried, cracked bark. This is a khejri. It hurts to see it and my eyes well with tears. Other fallen khejri surround it. And beyond them is a trench dug deep into the sand, filled with the corpses of more dead khejris.

'You see this land?'

Kailash sweeps a hand across the desert view. It holds low shrubs but no trees.

'Now see that land.'

He points to a long wall of cement blocks beyond which is land privately owned by a man who would not sell to the energy company. It is rich in tall khejri trees, spreading full crowns.

'The khejri trees you see there? All were here!'

This land where we are standing, now emptied of its trees, was once filled with them. The landowner made money by leasing his land to the energy company. A local government official whose job was to fill in the permit wrote that there were no khejri trees here, and then signed and submitted the form.

Had he been punished?

'Martin! He didn't even lose his job!'

The trees had been buried. Hidden from sight. Imagine the labour of that, and the guilt implied, huge workforces chopping down trees and grubbing up their roots, digging long deep trenches that they then fill with trees and cover up. Look, no trees!

Kailash and friends determined to dig them up as evidence of the slaughter that had happened here. Under pressure from the 'administration', the local government, nobody in the nearby towns would rent them a JCB to do the job.

So they brought in a digger from a hundred miles away in Bikaner.

The digger worked for five days at twenty burial sites.

'Martin, you want to see more khejri trees? Come!'

Our jeep stops at the site of another massacre. Each site was given a letter and each dead tree a number. This was site C. We stand beside tree C27, written in red.

Our arrival startles a white-footed fox that runs away, its ears large, its feet white, a broad white tip to its grey tail.

'Where can it live?' Kailash asks. The fox's habitat is now land denuded of its trees and plated with solar panels.

'Look, Martin, look.'

And Kailash leads me to a fallen khejri, its body laid beside another tree that was its companion in death. He bends down and reaches his arms right around it, stretching hard, but his hands are way short of meeting each other. This slow-growing tree is too old, too big, to fully hug. Tears wet his eyes and his voice shakes.

'Fifteen days I was here, day, night, on the ground, no mat, no pillow.'

'Did you eat?'

'I saw the trees. I was too upset to eat. I was hungry, but I can't see these trees and then want to eat.'

Others joined him. Bhagirath, the tall friend who farms nearby and sent Kailash the first alert, supplied them with food, water, a tent. This wasn't a matter of saving trees because it was too late for that. It was mounting vigil, guarding the evidence. They had dug up these trees. Nobody must take them away.

'They were still green when we dug them up, Martin,' Kailash says, his voice still shaking. And their running sap was the colour of blood. 'They were bleeding. Bleeding red.' The fingertips of Kailash's brown hands are curiously white and he traces a channel between the cracks in the tree's dried bark.

Khejris, the state tree of Rajasthan, are protected by law. If you're found to have illegally felled a tree you must plant ten more. In thirty years, if they survive, ten such khejris might just about begin to replace one with hundreds of years of growth in it.

In shrubby ground nearby Kailash showed me the site of the protest.

The 363 martyrs at Khejarli had streamed in from many Bishnoi villages to each hold onto a tree in the way Amrita Devi and her children had done, and each be killed. Here, three centuries later, Bishnoi villagers had packed into trucks and buses and rushed to the scene of another massacre site. Remember, Bishnois would rather die than let a tree be killed. And yet by the time they got here they were too late. Thousands of trees were already chopped down and buried.

A field full of corpses, of beheaded women and children, would have been the direst, most grievous thing, but this massacre of trees, great benign forces that could not protect themselves, was, for the Bishnois, even more horrific.

The protesters felt anger, but also huge grief.

Old men and women, children, priests, everybody, they lowered themselves to the ground where they spread their bodies flat. They pressed the palms of their hands against the desert sand. They had no trees to hug so they hugged the earth, and the emptiness of the trees that once grew here and made this a living desert.

Newspaper articles presented the protests as some sort of victory. The local municipality issued an order. In future, energy companies must protect the trees when setting the lines of solar panels in place, and relocate the trees to a different site if necessary. They did not suggest how you can safely transplant a tree with a root system that is a hundred feet deep.

They also pledged to investigate the illegal felling and burial of the khejris. The cases against Kailash and others who were arrested would be examined by someone with no vested interest in the issue. And they promised to send security officers to protect nearby households who had been threatened by those who wanted the power plant to steam ahead.

So this mass felling of khejris for the building of solar fields can't happen again?

'Oh it will, it will.'

The men all gather. They see no hope. They are just people, and they are up against international corporations and their government.

I suggest it is a legal matter. There was a false statement on the environmental impact assessment. The 2021 Google map of the area shows the khejri trees. The energy company had them dug up. A lawyer could use that evidence of previous malpractice to demand to see permits for all future planned solar fields, and make sure that any presence of khejris is noted and respected. Given the evidence of buried khejri trees uncovered by this band of Bishnois and their digger, a lawyer could also force the energy company to comply with the law that requires ten trees to be planted for every one cut down.

'Where are these lawyers?' the men ask.

'My forefathers died to protect these trees,' Kailash says, and looks toward the horizon. All the trees that were in view are now vanished.

We move back to the SUV. Bhagirath is at the wheel. He floors the accelerator and we roar away. Kailash puts his arm around me to pull me more firmly on the seat and holds me tight against him, protecting me from falling.

'Martin, I want to eat you,' he says.

'You want to eat me?'

He wants to cook me dinner. It came out wrong. We all laugh and bounce and sway across the desert where there are no more trees.

14

Passing Amrita Devi's Baton

TRAVEL THROUGH RAJASTHAN and it's obvious when you're in Bishnoi territory: the khejri trees are thick-crowned and flourishing. And then immediately they are sick things, their bared branches ending with rosettes of leaves like pompoms, and you know you are passing through neighbouring land where the farmers lop growth from the trees to provide fodder. And you wonder at human blindness, that the evidence of how you can profit by caring for your trees does not even cross the boundaries of Bishnoi land.

Here's good news though. A community may be stubborn and find it hard to change its ways, yet an individual can always break through. I imagine a baton carved of wood to resemble a tree, held by Amrita Devi and passed into the hands of others. Others like Gaura Devi.

In April 2011 Jairan Ramesh, then India's Environment Minister and now a prominent spokesman for environmental causes, commented that: 'Amrita Devi inspired Gaura Devi to lead a band of intrepid women to protect their trees in Reni village in Chamoli district of Uttarakhand in 1974, giving rise [more accurately, giving a boost and some world renown] to the famous Chipko movement. Thus two women, Amrita Devi and Gaura Devi, are the pioneers of the environmental conservation movement in our country.'[50] He inaugurated environmental awards in both their names.

Gaura Devi was born into a land of myth in 1925. Her birth village of Laka stands at an altitude of 7,000 feet, and from there a trail leads up to the twin Himalayan peaks of Nanda Devi. This is not just a mountain, but the villagers' presiding deity: Nanda Devi is one name given to the wife of the supreme god Shiva. Another is the name given to this baby girl: Gaura. The main temple to Nanda Devi was in Gaura Devi's village. Forests coated the lower flanks of the mountainside.

Those forests gave Gaura what she knew of schooling, not formal book learning but lessons in how people and trees support each other. Forests were 'considered a woman's *maika* (maternal home), because from woods to water, women relied on jungles for their everyday needs'.[51] When she was twelve, Gaura Devi moved across the river and married a farmer who reared sheep and traded wool in the village of Reni. At nineteen she had a son, Chandra. And at twenty-two her husband died. The young widow was left with a child and her in-laws to support.

Only men were allowed to plough, so she had to haggle with men to get them to do that job, taking on all other work herself. Her self-sufficiency made her stand out. In 1963 her village elected her head of their small Mahila Mangal Dal (Women's Welfare Group). Its main responsibility was to protect the forests and ensure that the village stayed clean.

In 1962, at the end of the Indo-Chinese war, trees started to be felled to build roads to ease military access. Eight years later, in 1970, severe floods swept the region. The locals recognised the role of trees in flood control.

Traditionally, villagers used wood from an ash grove to make their tools. In 1972 the authorities refused them permission to gather such wood, instead selling the ash trees to a sporting goods company. In protest, villagers gathered, sang folk songs, and hugged the trees. The ash grove was spared. The move helped form the Chipko movement, 'chipko' in Hindi meaning 'to cling to' or 'to stick to' – and so, with the trees, 'to hug'.

The wife and husband team Vimla and Sunderlal Bahaguna were among its leaders, working on Gandhian principles of non-violent intervention. They focused on forest conservation, eventually coming round to the Bishnoi stance that no living tree should be cut. 'Forests awake! Forest peoples awake!' became their slogan. A separate wing of the movement, led by Chandi Prasad Bhatt, focused on sustainable production to benefit forest-dependent communities.

This leader, Chandi Prasad Bhatt, attended the January 1974 auction of the Reni forest. His handwritten posters pointed out how the forestry department focused on revenue and not ecology. It made no difference. The forest was sold. He took his issues to lively meetings in villages of the area, including in Reni, where he explained the likelihood of floods if the forests were cut. Gaura Devi's son Chandra, now grown-up, was in the audience and took details back to his mother.

In March, when contractors were due to cut the forest, Chandi Prasad Bhatt intended to lead protests in Reni. Instead he was called away to a distant town for meetings with the District Forest Officer. It was a ploy to keep him out of the way.

The authorities deployed a second ruse to make sure there were no men around the village. Back in 1962, when some of their land was appropriated by the government in the wake of the Indo-Chinese war, the men of Reni were promised compensation. For fourteen years, no money came their way. Suddenly: 'Come to the city of Chimoli on March 26,' the men were told, 'and at last you will be paid due compensation.' And off they went.

At around 10am on 26 March 1974, contractors brought in by bus from Himachal, hidden behind drawn curtains, were driven to Reni. A jeep filled with forestry officials followed. Rather than taking the main road into the forest, the bus stopped short of the village. The men walked up a path from the banks of the Rishiganga. The plan had been to keep the operation secret, but a girl spotted the men and ran to find Gaura Devi. She was in the village cooking dinner, another woman was weaving, another bathing her child. Twenty-one women set aside their tasks and followed Gaura Devi up the track into the forest, with seven of their young daughters tagging along behind.

They found the labourers, their tools thrown onto the ground while they waited for their lunch to be cooked. The emergence from the forest of this group of women, dressed in vivid colours and gusting breaths from their brisk steep walk, shouting cries of defiance, came at the men like a supernatural force. The women's pleas flew at them from all sides. 'Don't cut our forest! It gives us our wood, our grass, our herbs, our vegetables. Cut it and the hills will fall on our village; great floods will sweep us to our deaths. Our farms beside the river will be washed away. This is our *maika*. Don't destroy our homes.' They saw the men were preparing their meal. 'Eat it,' the women said, 'and come back down with us.'

Some of the men were drunk. They shouted at the women, told them to clear off and leave them to work, threatened to have them arrested. One drunken forester had a gun. He raised it and stumbled toward the women.

'Here!' Gaura Devi shouted and started to unbutton her blouse. She was inviting the drunken forester to put a bullet through her heart. 'Shoot me and cut down my *maika* and take it away.' Her words stunned the men to silence. Again and again these women had spoken of their *maika*, this forest they viewed as their 'maternal home', one that gave them all they needed to live. You want to chop down a tree? Then first kill this woman. It is the same thing.

One man stepped forward and disarmed the drunken forester. Other labourers started to walk down the tracks. More women arrived from the village and turned around men they found bringing up the company's provisions. A photograph of the time shows women surrounding the thick trunk of a tree, their backs to it, facing out, their hands pressed against the tree's bark, 'sticking' close to the tree in the Chipko fashion.

Some women picked up iron staves left behind by the workers. Cement had been used to repair a section of the

road that had been stripped away by a landslide. With the staves, the woman broke up the cement and made the road impassable. Women and children sat at the beginning of the track into the forest, and into sunset and then throughout the night they sang songs in praise of Nanda Devi and other deities. The contractors called Gaura Devi to one side, threatened her, spat at her. She returned to sit guard, and to sing to the goddess.

The next morning Chandi Prasad Bhatt, the Chipko leader, arrived at Reni along with the returning male villagers. The women approached him, their hands clasped, and explained what they had done. 'What we did was the right thing to do,' Gaura Devi said. 'There was no violence, no one was hit. We spoke to them decently. If the police arrest us, we have no fear. We saved our *maika*, our fields, and our lands beside the river.'

Instinctively the women applied the Bishnoi rule of not speaking against people who are not there with you. They did not tell their menfolk about being threatened with a gun, about being spat at. It would have enflamed the situation and might have meant the Himachali labourers losing their jobs. Nobody wanted men to lose their jobs.

For four days, demonstrations were held where the labourers were gathered, Chandi Prasad Bhatt making speeches, many of the labourers sitting among the crowd that took in his words. The workforce began to drift away. The villagers kept watch.

At the end of 1977 the state government announced that the 2,451 trees that were set to be felled in Reni would not be cut. The following April, villagers from the surrounding hamlets poured into the village to celebrate the fourth anniversary of the women's action, and the success. They wore their traditional clothes, brought along their musical instruments, and sang and danced in celebration. 'I have saved my *maika*, my maternal home,' Gaura Devi told them, 'but there are many, many other *maikas* that still need to be saved.'

She took a lead role in supporting other activists protecting their forests. Shekhar Pathak, then a young activist who decades later went on to become the movement's historian, notes that while the women did not know the Gandhian or Marxist philosophies of the Chipko leaders, 'the promises that these leaders made remained promises until fulfilled by the unprecedented and momentous action by ordinary village women.'[52] Their success became headline news and spurred other groups of women to protect threatened forests. Reflecting on the women under Gaura Devi's leadership, the Chipko leader Vimla Bahaguna said that with their actions: 'Chipko became a women's movement. For the first time, the women took the lead without the men.'

When battling to save the environment, the trick is to celebrate victories but then go back to the fight, because forces of destruction never give up. Gaura Devi kept campaigning, but when she died aged sixty-six, after a paralysing illness, all had not gone well for her *maika*, her forest. The village of Reni stretched back from the banks of the Rishiganga, which now housed the Rishiganga Hydroelectric Project. On 7 February 2021 unusually high temperatures prompted the collapse of a glacier, which triggered a flash flood that destroyed the power plant and swept away the lower part of the village. Some 206 people were reported missing, and 88 bodies were recovered.

The villagers of Reni asked to be relocated. Nobody listened. Then on 17 June new floods hit them.

Reni resident Asha Devi Rana, who recalled taking part in Gaura Devi's days of action, lost her younger sister, Amrita Devi, to the floods. 'We were poor and needed money,' she recalls, remembering why she sold her land for the power plant to be built. 'But the price we paid for this dam is too much. It never gave us anything; now it has taken my sister from me. They have fooled us, they never told us what we were getting into.' The sense in the village is that, had the dam not been there, the change in the flow of the river would have given the villagers enough warning to flee.

Back in 1730, the men who wanted to chop down Amrita Devi's forest of khejri trees offered her a bribe. Today this might be called 'compensation'. Amrita Devi refused it. Reports from India state that men are ejecting women from village councils, so they can accept offers of roads and schools in exchange for the surrounding trees. The women, who wanted to reject such offers, leave the meetings and head to the forests to protect those trees. The forest is their 'mother'. It gives them life. They are not prepared to sell it.

Chandra Singh Rana, Gaura Devi's son, sees how life has changed. 'The generation of my mother was a selfless one. We are not like that. We are greedy. We wanted the money, we wanted the jobs. And today, we are paying the price for it. Our village is not habitable anymore, and our loved ones are dying.'[53]

Vandana Shiva, a quantum physicist and an eco-feminist voice, was schooled in environmental activism by her time in the Chipko movement. 'I learned how you have to turn within yourself to see what resources you have, rather than looking externally,' she recalls. She joined village women campaigning to stop the deforestation of their village under the slogan: 'What are the jungles' gifts? Soil, water and pure air'. This reclaimed the forest from the language of economics: words such as resin, timber and revenue.

Chipko taught Vandana Shiva ecology and biodiversity. In the wake of a devastating flood, when the women finally got logging banned, it was in part 'because the authorities finally understood what the women were saying: forests regulate water, and therefore to avoid floods and droughts, we need to protect our forests. While others had treated the forest as separate from the river, the women knew it was connected.' That was back in 1978, the year after the actions in Reni finally prompted a logging ban there. Now science is able to view forests in terms of their ecological functions. 'Scientists took half a century to catch up with illiterate women.'[54]

Regarding Amrita Devi and those Khejarli martyrs, Vandana Shiva writes: 'Today, as the ecological crisis deepens with forest fires in the Arctic, floods in the desert of Ladakh and in China and Pakistan, we can find renewed inspiration and a vision for the future from worldviews that see nature as alive and as the very basis of human life.'[55]

15

In This Together

THE BISHNOI BELIEVE IN SAVING THE PLANET, but they can't do it on their own. If billions of non-Bishnois all do their little bit, drop by drop ... who knows? Perhaps we could start using 'bishnoi' as an adjective in the way 'zen' is used: this project is very 'bishnoi'. It takes care of nature.

Back in 1983, in the Kanpur district of Uttar Pradesh, the state to the east of Rajasthan, poachers were targeting nilgai, those large antelopes who are fond of eating crops. On 26 April, a twenty-three-year-old man – a non-Bishnoi – announced that in fifteen days he would set himself alight if this nilgai poaching was not stopped.

Nobody responded. On 11 May, Harinarayana Bajpai duly settled himself down on the banks of the river Saigur and burned himself to death.

The Bishnoi read about his actions and took his cause as their own. They sent reports of the incident to government officials and awaited responses.

None came.

So they announced that one Bishnoi a day would sit where Harinarayana had sat and follow his example, set themselves alight, until action was taken.

Their deadline neared.

On 13 August, the state government of Uttar Pradesh announced the banning of many forms of hunting.[56]

One man burns himself to death? Well, that's one protester less. One nuisance despatched.

One Bishnoi threatens to die for a cause? The authorities know the problem will escalate until it is solved.

Now a leading elder in the conservation movement, Harsh Vardhan was working as an environmental journalist in 1976. After a reporting mission in Jodhpur, he had a free day before his evening train. With a driver and a photographer he headed out in search of chinkara. He spotted the animals, but the local Bishnoi also spotted him. First they shouted their challenges. And when the chinkara fled for the safety of the village and Harsh and his small party gave chase, the villagers blocked the road and wielded batons. An argument flared at the front of the jeep while Bishnoi men rummaged through the back of the vehicle in search of guns.

The driver spoke the villagers' dialect. His passengers were not hunters, he explained, but a reporter and a photographer, who shot with a camera not a gun.

The aggression melted. The villagers became happy to field questions. In response to one, a young man led Harsh toward his hut. Within, a young woman wearing a veil was squatting in a corner, a baby chinkara by her side. The young man spoke to her. She bared her breast and guided the chinkara's mouth to her nipple. Poachers from the city had killed its mother a few days before, and then fled. The Bishnoi woman was acting as its mother.

On the train that night Harsh kept waking. Each time he did, the image of the woman breastfeeding the orphaned chinkara shone vivid before him. 'She is around me even today; in thoughts at least,' Harsh recalled. 'I was enslaved by these people.'[57]

In December 1978 an Arab prince and his retinue crossed from Pakistan to camp in the Thar Desert outside Jaisalmer. They were there to shoot Great Indian Bustards. A group of villagers marched in protest through the streets of Jaisalmer and, alerted to the situation, Harsh marched too. 'When there's a breach of the Wildlife Act, and the government is not doing anything, we have to stand in opposition,' he recalls. 'It fell on our shoulders. You write a letter, the government does nothing. The only thing you can do is protest in the street.'

The march was in Jaipur, where Harsh supplied a group of forty Bishnoi with banners painted with slogans and led them to the home of the governor. The mansion served as a scenic backdrop for a photo opportunity. Journalists had received Harsh's press release. 'The press is a messenger,' Harsh explains. 'A bridge between society and the rest of the world. The worth of the media was known to me.'

The Jaipur protest against the royal hunting party became the front-page story in the following morning's edition of the newspaper *Patrika*. It served as a lesson for the Bishnoi in how to deploy the media in support of their aims; each action for wildlife becomes a campaign.[58]

Harsh Vardhan pioneered another conservation campaign method the Bishnoi would utilise: use of the courts to protect wildlife. With a friend in Jodhpur, he petitioned the Rajasthan High Court to stop the Arab hunting party and on New Year's Day 1979, the court took mere minutes to deliver its decision; they imposed an immediate fourteen-day ban on killing bustards in the Thar Desert. The Arab hunting party withdrew.

Isn't it expensive, I ask Harsh, taking your wildlife cases to court?

'I've given petitions to court four times, and never used a lawyer,' he says. 'In any case, I couldn't afford one. I have faith.'

When the Bishnoi caught Salman Khan hunting black-buck, Harsh took their case to Dourdarshan TV. At the time, he had a high-powered management job running PR for a major company that relied on its government contracts. 'I bitterly criticised the Chief Minister's Office – they were just sitting on this poaching case. My action was picked up as evidence against me. I was a threat to the government.'

His activism cost Harsh his job. Since then he's got by on his passion for wildlife.

Whenever I read reports about nature conservation in India, Harsh's name crops up. For example when the Indian government memorialised the sacrifice of villagers in the 1730 massacre at Khejarli, on the 2001 anniversary, it was marked by the presentation of the annual Amrita Devi Bishnoi Wildlife Protection Award. This is given for a sig-nificant act of nature conservation and that first award was posthumous, to Ganga Ram Bishnoi from the village of

Chirai who was shot in 2000 while chasing deer hunters. 'Financial help was offered to his widow,' I read, 'by Mr. Harsh Vardhan.'

Money, for Harsh, is a free-flowing stream; you don't build a dam and collect it but direct it to whatever needs watering. His sense of money reflects the words of Jambhoji. 'If you have something in little quantity, donate little; do not refuse to donate if you have something.' Harsh has a simple policy as regards finances. 'We should save as much as we can and put all that into conservation. Be truthful to yourself and to society or we become hypocrites. Money makes us a different person. I need it, but I am doing conservation work without it.'

A decade or so ago, when Harsh was on an overnight business trip in Jodhpur, the Bishnoi asked him to join in a protest against chinkara hunting. He did. 'I spoke loudly, and didn't know what consequences would happen.' The police charged him with 'violating civic norms' and the case continues. Ram Niwas, who guided me on my initial excursions into the Bishnoi world, has a dozen such cases against him, Harsh tells me. Jail is a constant threat.

Back in Jodhpur, I meet with Ram Niwas to find out how his environmental activism has evolved in the face of so many legal threats.

Simply put, his thinking has evolved in this way: if you believe in the law, and you want the law to work for you in saving the planet, then become your own lawyer. Many young Bishnois have taken up legal studies, and Ram Niwas too. He now has both a Bachelors and a Masters degree in

Law. These Bishnois don't carry guns but they are armed with the law: in protecting nature, it's not about their own sense of justice, but about what the law allows and what it forbids. That's what they can enforce. If they are too late to stop the natural world being harmed, then they can collect and protect evidence, and make sure those who inflict damage on the natural world are punished as an example to others.

'Normally we reach an incident before the forestry department,' Ram Niwas says, 'but if they get there first, people will tell them to wait till the Bishnoi arrive. They have such awareness and confidence in our work. The officers ask us what laws apply. There is trust for us among the people. Now we say to the police, "We are with you. We are doing your job. All you have to do is the paperwork."'

This new band of activist-lawyer-Bishnoi do legal work to protect the *orans* too, those areas of village land set aside as preserves for nature and pasture. 'We want to make the government register them – their records are inaccurate. We've helped a man draft a successful action against the government for giving this pastureland away.'

What about all these actions against him that are still working through the courts – how does he feel about them?

His face flushes, his eyes moisten: 'When an animal feels harm, the pain that causes us puts us through so much more than the police could ever give us.'

These Bishnoi lawyers extend their expertise into other communities who battle to protect the natural world that surrounds them.

Landlocked in Central India, the state of Chhattisgarh has a tropical climate and is known as being 'rich in resources', which makes it vulnerable to exploitation. Among Indian states it has the third-largest coal deposits, and forty per cent of its land is covered in trees, much of it within the Hasdeo forest. When you add the forested lands in the neighbouring states, the Hasdeo is the largest contiguous forest in India. It covers 170,000 hectares of Chhattisgarh alone and provides migratory routes for herds of elephants, as well as being home to tigers and leopards and sloth bears, and to four hundred and six species of birds. Groups of India's indigenous peoples, including the Gond, Oraon and Lohar communities, know this forest as their home.

Citing its rich biodiversity and high ecological value, Chhattisgarh's Ministry of Coal and Ministry of Forest and Environment declared the Hasdeo Reserve a 'No Go Area' in 2010, banning any kind of mining. Sadly, cheap coal extraction often trumps nature protection. A Rajasthan government-owned electricity company owned the mining rights to the Parsa East Kete Basan coal mine, within the reserve, and in 2011 licensed them to the Adani corporation, one of India's largest companies, which retains and exploits an immense stake in global coal production. By 2013, vast swathes of forest had become open-cast mines.

Survival International reports how indigenous women lead fights to protect forests, because 'their land is their life: the center of their cultural, economic, spiritual existence and the central source of their subsistence and livelihood'. They have been facing this threat for decades. In the neighbouring state of Odisha in the 1980s, 'women put their babies on the road

in front of the police and bulldozers to show that future generations' lives depend totally on stopping the mines.'[59]

In 2024, on the fiftieth anniversary of Gaura Devi's
actions, *Nature* magazine noted how 'hundreds of Chipko-
like movements have bloomed in villages and cities across
India, inspired by a simple idea – hugging a tree to save
it – and by the courage of village folk.'[60] In 2022 hundreds
of members of indigenous groups had begun months-long
sit-ins to save the Hasdeo forest from being felled, women
following Amrita Devi's and Gaura Devi's example and
clutching hold of trees. 'We are from the jungle,' one of these
women said, already two months into her night-and-day
protection of the trees. 'Our entire livelihood depends on it.
If this forest is destroyed, then the tribals* who have lived in
this area for centuries will also be uprooted. Even if we lose
our lives, we will not let coal mining happen here.'[61]

They are increasingly on their own. A government law bans
the use of foreign funds to support environmental litigation
in India. On 7 September 2022, Indian government tax
officials raided the offices of several Indian environmental
NGOs, including India's foremost environmental law NGO,
the Legal Initiative for Forest and Environment (LIFE). The
intimidation had an effect. On 26 September, lawyers from
LIFE wrote to an indigenous leader, withdrawing from the
lawsuit to save the Hasdeo forest. On the same day, logging

---

* More than 8 per cent of India's population belongs to what the Indian
Government terms 'Scheduled Tribes'. In the 1930s indigenous activists
adopted the Sanskrit word *Adivasi* as a collective name for the tribal groups
of the Indian sub-continent. While many groups use that term, those in this
area still use the word tribal.

crews started to clear 106 acres of forest for the Phase 2 expansion of the Adani mines. In October the logging was paused as the case moved to India's Supreme Court. If it resumes, 2,700 acres will be lost.[62] In early 2023, Indian authorities froze the foreign-currency bank account of LIFE, which gets 75–80 per cent of its budget from foreign donations. Six of its eight staff members lost their jobs. The indigenous peoples of Hasdeo claim that papers granting their consent to the mining were forged.

'We have faith in the courts,' one villager says. 'This isn't just a fight for Hasdeo. We are fighting for this country and for the world, which is staring at the dangers of climate change and environmental degradation.'[63] But who is left to help them navigate legal hurdles to save their forest lands?

'We are there,' Ram Niwas tells me. 'Five members of the Bishnoi Tiger Force have been deployed to help the women save the forest. Tribal women are in hospital having got injured. We are guiding the local Bishnois with the law from Jodhpur, but if needed we will go.'

16

Bishnoi Tiger Force

ON A HILL ON THE FRINGES OF JODHPUR, in a fenced compound planted with trees, I meet with men of the Bishnoi Tiger Force. The conversation is orderly, and each speaker starts with a shout, punches the air, and boosts the volume from there.

'We have a campaign! We want the government to impose ten- to fifteen-year prison sentences for the illegal cutting of trees, and on top of that, a hundred thousand rupee fine!'

'Now the law says that for each tree cut down, ten more should be planted! It's not enough! This should be twenty new trees planted! And this should be a worldwide rule – plant twenty trees for every one cut! Jambhoji's rules are not just for Bishnois – they are for all humans!'

Ram Niwas does what he always does when conversation gets heated: he smiles softly. And when he speaks, his explanations sooth things. 'We lead movements wherever possible. Our campaigns led to a chapter on Amrita Devi being included in school textbooks. And because of our campaigning, punishments for infringements of the 1972 Wildlife Protection Act have been made more severe. We are currently arguing for environmental topics to be added to the school curriculum. And also that TV adverts should include five to ten seconds about the environment and our need to save trees.'

And now I learn about the Bishnoi Tiger Force's current campaign. A stretch of new highway runs a partial ring around the city, seemingly from nowhere to nowhere. In time it will be a ring road but for now work has stopped. And it won't resume until the Bishnoi Tiger Force receives proof that the trees in the area are being shown proper care, that they are only cut down when it is absolutely necessary, and are transplanted when that is possible.

How did they manage that?

'Peaceful protest,' Ram Niwas says. 'We just go and sit on the site and tell the people working there what they should be doing.'

How could a few men turning up and sitting down bring an ongoing mega project to a halt?

Heads tilt, surprised at my puzzlement. 'These construction crews know the Bishnoi,' they tell me. 'OK, there are only a few of us at first. But if there's no response to our demands, in an hour there will be a hundred people.'

'Then a thousand,' says another.

'Then ten thousand.'

The Bishnoi are relentless. Their commitment to a cause isn't time sensitive, taken as a break from their regular lives; it becomes their life. The examples of their pursuit of Salman Khan, of the actions of Amrita Devi and the martyrs of Khejarli, and the unarmed men who take on armed poachers, prove their boundless will to fight. When Bishnois stand in the way of your project, it's time to reconsider your approach.

The religious order of the Jains, who are also prominent in Rajasthan, seems akin to the Bishnoi religion. They wear masks to make sure they kill no insect by breathing it in, and sweep the ground so they tread nothing to death. They also maintain animal shelters and scatter food for great flocks of demoiselle cranes in winter, as the Bishnoi do on the dune where we are having this meeting. 'Non-violence in Jainism ... is a proactive principle that asks us to act and live in such a way so as to reduce the amount of harm that takes place in the world,' the Vedic scholar David Frawley writes.[64]

How do the two groups differ?

The Jains form of ultimate self-sacrifice is *Sallekhana,* whereby followers attain their ideal death by fasting: asking nothing of the world in this way means doing no injury to it and severing all ties. For the Bishnoi, self-sacrifice is often instinctive, a passionate engagement with the world, putting their lives on the line when they see nature as vulnerable.

The Jains have their origins much further back in time, the Bishnois explain. They tend to be wealthier and live largely in cities, whereas Jambhoji gave the Bishnoi practices that work in villages. He taught them to chant the name of Vishnu, but to do so out in the fields, where they were working. Their religious practice was community-wide and enfolded in an agrarian life. This meant that the Bishnoi never separated themselves from wild animals and trees but lived alongside

them. Because they never separated from the natural world, and are fully identified with all that grows around them, their words assume power. 'Stop,' they can say to the person cutting down a tree. 'Don't you see? You are cutting down yourself.'

Ram Niwas puts it simply. 'If we feel that a tree is our child, that feeling will be opened to others.'

What might they get back from helping nature?

'We don't think about it. From birth it's what we do. It's who we are. Our practices define us.' And then he thinks on, wondering about the years he has dedicated to the work of the Tiger Force. Yes, there's benefit there. 'We get to meet people – that is what we get. Amongst all communities, our identity is linked to protecting nature.'

With us is the All India President of the Bishnoi Tiger Force, Rampal Bhawat Bishnoi. Back in 1995, he was one of the founding members of the Force. His hair is still dark yet thin and slicked back, and his presence in the group till now has been solid and benign yet silent. Now he responds to a direct question. He started by fighting poachers. Yet today nobody is talking about poachers and everyone is talking about trees.

'How come?' I ask him.

'Poaching used to be the big problem, but now not so much. That's largely because of our success against Salman Khan. Now, with the building of highways and developments it's the loss of trees.'

By developments, he includes the swathes of land that abut the highways for miles out of Jodhpur, surrounded by low walls and set to become new housing estates.

'We're not against development, but we don't want it to replace the environment.'

A cry goes up, men turning and shouting and pointing: a few chinkara are seen, at first grazing, but then they are running, and a dog races into view, barking, and men jump from the sand and break from the group, yelling at the dog to stop its attack, chasing after it.

Om Prakash was first to that chase. His farm is on the outskirts of Jodhpur, but one call to his phone will see him rush to a cause. A string of beads is tight around his thick neck. On the way to our conversation, he and Ram Niwas engaged in a playful tussle, Om Prakash landing real blows. 'He keeps fighting me,' Ram Niwas says. Does he hurt you? 'Yes!'

Om Prakash returns to the group and tells a story. He saw two army officers in town, trading blows, the fight growing dangerous. The police came by and needed a witness. Several men who had watched the fight slunk away. Om Prakash stepped forward.

'Why do that?' his friends asked him.

'I had to,' he told them. 'It's one of our twenty-nine rules. You must speak the truth.'

Opening his phone, he shows a scene from a recent flash flood. One man is in a fast stream of floodwater that is roaring down a deep cement channel. With his right hand and arm he presses a chinkara close to his chest. His left arm is stretched its full length, his hand clasped by a man leaning over the trench's side, his arm too at full stretch, the water heaving past below them while they wait for a ladder to be brought to rescue both man and chinkara. This is the

Bishnoi Tiger Force in action, rescuing a tiny gazelle that others might have watched spin away to its drowning.

'We are all volunteers,' Ram Niwas reminds me. 'We respond to incidents, then go back to our activities. All across India, communities are trying to establish an identity for themselves. Bishnoi youth are not trying to create an identity for themselves, but to present our religion and practices. Other Bishnoi associations have won government awards, but the Tiger Force's impact in a short time has been much more. We know that we are not alone. Our whole community is behind us. Our religion gives us confidence.'

The time comes for a group Tiger Force photograph. The men stand in a line and Rampal Bhawat Bishnoi, their All India President, opens his mouth and roars. 'Jai Jambheshwar!'

Jai, means 'Victory' and also 'Hail' and 'All praise'. *Jambheshwar* is the name that carries the divine status of their guru, Jambhoji.

'Jai Jambheshwar!' goes up a deafening group shout.

'Jai Amrita Devi!'

It's call and response, loud and thrilling.

'Jai Amrita Devi!'

'Jai the three hundred and sixty-three martyrs!'

'Jai all those who died saving animals and trees!'

And in the charge of their shouts, the spirits of those who have gone before them, who have given their lives to save others, infuse them. The group breaks up, each man to his family and his daily life, but the sense of mission has been strengthened and the group stays bound.

In their fierceness of spirit these men of the Bishnoi Tiger Force have a sixteenth-century precedent, a man designated by Jambhoji to be his successor. One who became known as 'The Enforcer'. A short journey east of Jodhpur brings you to his resting place.

108 श्री बील्हाजी महाराज

17

The Enforcer

EARLY MONSOON RAINS HAVE BEEN HEAVY and grasses are tall. A young cow drinks from a round stone trough brim-full of water. 'There!' a man calls and we watch an Indian hare race up a hillside. Inside a square of fencing, birds peck at grain scattered across the ground.

This is an *oran*, a wildlife preserve on the edge of the village of Ramrawas Kalan, a short drive east of Jodhpur. The land slopes down toward a lake, footprints of wild boar freshly pressed into the mud near its shore. 'The lake is three hundred and thirty-one years old,' one villager, a teacher, tells me, the knowledge a part of village lore because it was dug as an act of devotion by a local Bishnoi. 'It's here to give water to the blackbuck and chinkara. When it dries in summer we get a tractor and bring some water down here so that the smaller animals – wolves, foxes, hares and rabbits – can drink.'

But, surely, wolves might eat the chinkara?

'Jambhoji taught us to save all animals,' the teacher answers, 'from tiny insects to the largest. Wild boars aren't helpful to us, but we don't let them die. We do especially care for chinkara because they are beautiful, vulnerable, and there is nobody to care for them in this world. When dogs are hunting chinkara, we stop them. When people are hunting dogs, we stop them.'

'This is sacred land,' an older man in a white turban tells me, and with his hands directs me to look through 360 degrees. 'It is a mystical place. Back in the sixteenth century poachers were about to kill some deer. Suddenly the colour of the animals turned from brown to saffron, the same colour as the robes of our priests and of Jambhoji. The poachers froze. They could not shoot. They turned around and ran away.'

This summer's temperatures broke records, shooting beyond 50 degrees Celsius. We head for the shade of a distant khejri tree. How noticeable are the effects of climate change at this village level?

Three men pick up the question.

'There used to be many more windstorms. Each heavy wind was a prelude to monsoon rains sweeping in. Now there are few.'

'Yes. When you saw lightning and heard thunder in the north, rain was guaranteed. Now that's not so at all.'

'When it rained, it used to rain across the whole region. Now it's piecemeal, some rain here, nothing there.'

And what will they do if summer temperatures keep reaching record highs?

'More than five hundred years ago, Jambhoji taught us that if we don't plant trees our land will be too hot,' the teacher says. 'That message is still applicable. Even our government is now saying to plant and protect trees. Some people believe we can leave everything in the care of God, in the hands of Jambhoji, who will protect us and all will be well. But we do feel it is getting hotter, and feel if it becomes too hot we won't be able to do our agriculture. What can we do? We plant trees, especially in the rainy season of July and August. Even if only ten per cent survive, it will be good. We definitely have more trees now than we used to.'

'We are satisfied within ourselves,' the white-turbaned man adds, 'happy in our culture, and to be self-sufficient we grow our own crops. Even in families where they have jobs, they follow these village practices.'

The men's village is famed for being the adopted home of the foremost follower of Jambhoji.

It's hard to know what to make of Vilhoji. 'The important thing,' villagers explain to me, 'is that Jambhoji gave us the twenty-nine rules, and Vilhoji said you have to follow them. He was the enforcer.'

Vilhoji spent his last years here in this village, Ramrawas Kalan, and is entombed in a new, intricately carved sandstone temple. His sarcophagus – also new, yet with its top already polished by human touch – is carved in white marble in precise detail. Its image is that of the four-armed god, Vishnu.

'Vilhoji died on this spot in 1616, four hundred and seven years ago,' the temple's priest says, and draws the saffron cloth back over the sarcophagus. The priest wears full saffron himself, his short body permanently bent,

his dark eyes shining. 'He's buried fifteen feet down. For centuries his grave was just a shallow depression in the land, with a slab laid on top of it.'

Leaning on a wall behind the sarcophagus are paintings that portray both Vilhoji and Jambhoji. Vilhoji is shown as a young man, bare-chested, wearing a white wrap-around lunghi, a long string of beads hanging around his neck, his shaven head topped by a turban. In one painting a beam of light streams out of Jambhoji's clasped hands to form a halo around the young man's head, denoting a passing of the light from the founding guru to a successor.

If we are to take Jambhoji as being the eleventh incarnation of the god Vishnu, should we then take Vilhoji as the twelfth?[65]

'Absolutely,' the priest says. 'And here's how strong the man was. Jambhoji told us we must not kill. Vilhoji taught us further, that we must not even kill the lice on our heads. We must treasure all life.'

Vilhoji is credited with writing the texts which collect Jambhoji's teachings, while tales of his own life have been passed down as oral history. Here's a simple version.

Vilhoji was born in 1532 in the market town of Rewari, just south of Rajasthan. He was known then as Vithal. At the age of four, the boy lost his sight. At the same time, knowing that he was dying, Jambhoji appointed four priests to be his successors. Three were with him; another, he said, now unknown to them, would join them in future years. The child to whom he referred had been born to a carpenter's family, Jambhoji said, and he identified him by name as Vithal. He set aside robes for the boy, who would be revered as Vilhoji.

Though the boy was blind, read him a passage from a book just once and it was lodged word-perfect in his memory. It was the same with songs that he heard. He was five, singing a devotional song of love, when a passing sadhu heard his voice. The sound was sweet and utterly pure. The sadhu approached the boy's father. Might this blind boy join the sadhu's group, and travel with them?

Permission was given. Years passed and the boy grew up in the sadhu's company. They were on a pilgrimage to the famed city of Dwarka, which is known as the home of Krishna. Their route saw them pause near Mukam. Vithal set out on his morning walk, which brought him close to the temple where Jambhoji was buried.

A *havan* was being performed; Vithal could smell the smoke from its fire and heard Jambhoji's words being chanted by the crowd. 'I will stop here,' he told the sadhu, no longer needing to continue to Krishna's town of Dwarka. 'This is my Dwarka.'

Vithal spent time at the temple, took in the teachings, and asked to become a Bishnoi. Nathoji, one of the early disciples, brought him the water that has been rendered sacred by chanting over it the words of Jambhoji, the 'Pahul' of Bishnoi initiation. As the water passed through his mouth to his throat, the sight was restored to his eyes.

Was this the successor, Vilhoji, as prophesied by Jambhoji? In awe of the miracle they had witnessed, these early Bishnois asked the question. A king was present among them. 'You think you have the powers to take on such a task?' he challenged the young man. 'Give us evidence. Show us your powers.'

What could a villager do to impress a king? He reached into his bag ... and brought out a watermelon. Watermelons were out of season. No king's gold could buy one. Fresh heads of *bajra* (pearl millet) were not yet in season either. Yet the young man had reached into his bag and there, in his hand, was fresh *bajra*.

The king was convinced. To show his respect, he presented the young man – hereafter Vilhoji – with a whip – a fine tool for the 'enforcer' of Bishnoism. Other kings were impressed by Vilhoji's scholarship, and one, Maharajah Sur Singh, not only provided tents and equipment for his travels, but gave him the authority to administer punishment.

Vilhoji was not a missionary. Entering one village and finding its people fighting with each other and screaming curses, sooner than teach them better ways, he left. 'Where people are full of themselves, always quarrelling, foul-mouthed, speaking behind each other's backs, working to do harm, don't stay there,' he said. 'Not even for half an hour.'

Other places, where Bishnois lived, were different. If people there were swearing, arguing, breaking any of the twenty-nine rules they had sworn to live by, then they had to be brought back on track. Vilhoji the enforcer made use of his powers to punish, as well as the whip that he had been given. Wayward Bishnois were tied to a tree, where he flogged them.

'That whipping of bad Bishnois is a good, shocking, detail,' I tell twenty men, who sit in the shade of a khejri tree on the edge of Ramrawas village. 'It's fierce. Vilhoji was fierce. He shows typical Bishnoi power.'

The men laugh and clap their hands. 'It's true! And we are still fierce. But now we wouldn't tie them and beat them,' they say. 'We would cast them out.'

18

Preparing for War

THE STREETS OF JODHPUR GROW TIGHT, pedestrians outpace the clogged traffic of diesel vehicles, and Ram Niwas is driving us through it like a bumble bee, not wanting to be stuck in a city any more than I do. The road widens, and we start to climb the hill that holds Jodhpur's fort.

Jodhpur is known for its bright blue roofs and it's a relief to be above them where trees still have space to grow. But as with the building of the ring road, development threatens the natural world. 'They're building a new road around this hill, and were going to cut over a hundred trees,' Ram Niwas tells me. 'We went to the Collector.' He's the government official in charge of the district's revenue collection and of law and order. 'He agreed that chopping down so many trees was not a good idea. Surveys then worked out an alternative route in which only five trees were cut.'

He parks the car and leads me to a wooden gate within a stone wall. Prasan Puri Goswami opens it, as if the gate is a portal and he is the old green wizard ushering us into his realm. Mehrangarh Fort crowns the hill above, and seven and a half hectares of the hill's slopes hold land that he has turned into a medicine garden. We're coming back here at my request, two years after my first visit.

The garden began as a retirement project in 2007, after Prasan's lifetime's work as a history teacher, but the ambition was set in childhood, when he was saddened to see this hillside bare of life. He conjured visions of the slopes being planted with trees.

In 1987, when posted to a nearby girls' school, he planted saplings at a junction near the fort, and after school would ferry water to them from two ponds. At first people laughed at his labours, then some pupils and locals joined in. His work drew the attention of the district administration and the former royals who had custodianship of the fort. Would he care to plant trees on fifteen fenced-off hectares of the fort's hillside?

He would. He set about it. Tree by tree. It's surprising how many trees a piece of land can absorb without becoming dense forest. When he was a child this hill was bare. As an old man, he can look out on the fifty thousand trees he has planted.

When posted to a distant school he left his older son, Pramod, then aged twenty-eight, in charge. Pramod noticed a tree suffering rot and sprayed it with pesticide. Wind blew the poisons into his face, he collapsed, and died.

'I was shattered and thought of giving up,' Mr Goswami recalls. Then his mind turned to the trees. 'I thought, I have lost one son but what about the thousands of sons that I have planted and grown? So I decided that I must continue to take care of my plants. I see my son's image in them. I will always protect them.'

When necessary, they now use bio-pesticides that are not harmful to humans. The hillside is organic. In the side garden that constitutes his nursery, spokes of aloe vera fill one patch. Saplings are kept in terracotta pots for a year, to make sure they can survive in these surroundings, and only then are they planted.

Holes that Mr Goswami has dug in the ground fill with water in the period of monsoon. From that supply he can water trees for up to six months. In the heat of summer, before the rains come, he carries thirty litres of water a week to each tree. Some long narrow trenches, also dug by him, channel water down the hillside from the crenelated fortress walls at the top. This helps the grasses grow, and that brings the butterflies, and that brings the birds, and that brings eagles. In the summer, some five hundred people visit each day, on family outings, when they 'come to breathe oxygen and learn that trees are what we need to protect'.

Wildlife is returning, including porcupine. There are six species of snakes, including the krait, a small snake even more poisonous than a black cobra.

Vinodpuri, Mr Goswami's younger son, joins us. A self-taught naturalist, he is now the forester in charge of the seventy hectares of land inside the fort, an area being rewilded as an ecotourist destination. Botanists head out into rocky areas of the Thar and bring back seeds to grow here, or soil containing seeds of sewan grass (particularly suited to arid regions with 8–10 per cent protein in its early growth) to spread on the hillside. They plant in the monsoon season, water for seven-eight months, and that's it. 'There's no use having trees if you water them – this is a desert.'

'Look!' Vinodpuri runs me around a shrub to a tree where I find the bird just as it breaks into flight, a Jacobin cuckoo, black but for a white bib then brilliant white flashes in its tail and wings.

'A pair of white-browed wagtails come and sing here in the mornings, and I join in,' Vinodpuri says. 'We sing together.'

He plunges my nose into bushes to smell the flowers and hear the buzz of bees.

'A begonia,' he says. '*Corbichonia*, known as the four o'clock flower because that's when it opens its bright red blooms, but we also have ones that bloom white, so rare that botanists come here to study them.' And he prompts me to focus on the singing of red-vented bulbuls, then directs my gaze upward toward a Shikra, a grey bird of prey, atop a rock.

Ram Niwas loves nature but is blinkered when it comes to trees. He loves the ones beloved of Jambhoji. 'Kankeri!' he calls out in front of a tree that is about his height only thinner, the same species of tree under which Jambhoji took shelter on his dune retreat.

Ram Niwas's phone rings and he doesn't answer it with any normal hello: 'Jambhoji Bishnoi Bhagwan,' he asserts, the 'Bhagwan' translatable as Lord, denoting Jambhoji as an avatar of the god Vishnu.

My previous visit here was impromptu. This one is planned. 'We will plant a tree,' Mr Goswami tells me. 'To give you an emotional attachment. You will want to come back and see how it is doing.'

My sapling is of a small tree, *Anogeissus pendula*, with silver and grey bark. Its hole is dug and we plant it in a group ceremony before pouring in water.

'Do you feel like a Bishnoi?' I ask Mr Goswami.

He laughs. 'Bishnois have rules that say plant trees and save animals. So yes, I feel like a Bishnoi. Anyone who plants trees and saves animals is a Bishnoi.'

'Is that right?' I ask Ram Niwas.

'Yes,' and he gives a vigorous nod of his head.

Even so I sense concern as we walk away together, along a path. My trip is drawing to a close, and perhaps he is wondering why I asked to return here rather than to a specifically Bishnoi project. 'I asked to come back here to show how the Bishnoi are not closed,' I explain, 'but open to everybody who gives their life to protect the natural world.'

'Yes, yes,' and Ram Niwas grins, and takes my hand and shakes it firmly.

Ram Niwas doesn't own a car: to drive me around on each of our trips, he borrows one.

Previously the Bishnoi herded cattle and goats. Now trucks on the highway are decorated with pictures of Jambhoji, of chinkara, of Bishnoi slogans, as their drivers blast their horns and the engines belch out fumes. Bishnois have become known for running trucking businesses. They run the fleets of trucks that are polluting the environment. How do they square this with Jambhoji's teachings?

Ram Niwas brings in a historical perspective. 'At the end of the British Empire, the government made lists of caste groups. They ranked Bishnois as a caste, the government seeing us as backward, and so we have to raise ourselves. Previously we stayed in the fields like you said, and did our practices, and we got left behind. We can't get left behind, hence our involvement in the likes of trucking. As far as pollution goes, we follow the government rules.'

He clearly runs no such trucks himself. What does he do for income?

His answer involves all the family's adult males, showing that family income is shared. 'My father is a retired government officer and so he has his pension. My youngest brother runs the school. And I work as a legal consultant to a couple of local companies. I was elected head of the youth wing of the Congress party for the Jodhpur district.'

The younger brother is Narendra Bishnoi. The Saviour Children's Academy that they run together, which provides affordable schooling in English for rural Bishnoi, is a family operation but not a profit-making business. Its income doesn't cover its outgoings in terms of teacher's wages. Narendra's work as head teacher is essentially volunteer work; to support both the school and his wider family he doubles up with teaching jobs in the government system, and at weekends he heads back to the government school grounds, helping to take care of trees. A new tree is planted in the name of each child who joins the school, and child and tree then grow together. One day, as I watch at close of school, a girl pauses to pour water from her flask onto the roots of her tree.

The Saviour's Academy, where I first met Bishnoi children in February 2020, was closed a month later and didn't reopen for two years. India linked with the rest of the world in fighting the Covid pandemic. Narendra posted lockdown lessons on Facebook for the children to study at home.

His lessons were reflective. He saw the world as beset by inner and outer violence: outer violence includes war; inner violence includes harbouring feelings of hatred for others. 'There is enormous violence in the world,' he wrote, 'the rich wanting to keep people poor and the poor wanting to get rich and in the process hating the rich. And you,' he told the children, 'being caught in society, are also going to contribute to this.' He pulled no punches: 'You are still young but as you grow older you will realise how inwardly man goes through hell, goes through great misery, because he is in constant battle with himself, with his wife, with his children, with his neighbours, with his gods. He is in sorrow and confusion and there is no love, no kindliness, no generosity, and no charity.'

The girls in this virtual schoolroom could take this as a critique of men, or regender the advice. What was the challenge to these schoolchildren? 'Not to understand violence is to be really ignorant, is to be without intelligence and without culture. Life is something enormous, and merely to carve out a little hole for oneself and remain in that little hole, fighting off everybody, is not to live. It is up to you. From now on you have to know about all these things. You have to choose deliberately to go the way of violence or to stand up against society.'

There's a simple choice: society offers a way of violence. It needs to be resisted. What then?

'Be free, live happily, joyously, without any antagonism, without any hate. Then life becomes something quite different. Then life has a meaning, is full of joy and clarity.'

This is unlike any education I can remember. It sets up a conversation with Ram Niwas, as he reflects on how Bishnoi children are being prepared as leaders for a time of future conflict.

On our final trip, Ram Niwas takes a smart new highway out of the city. To one side, below the raised road, the scene is picturesque. Trees stand on small islands in what looks like a lake. In fact it's a field flooded by recent heavy monsoon rains. Ram Niwas shakes his head as he explains the sad situation. The field was illegally mined by constructors to supply the sand with which the road was built. As a result the fields flooded. The natural ponds that lie just beyond, on which the local people and animals depend, have lost their catchment. They stand dry.

The sight puts Ram Niwas into ruminative mode.

'Jambhoji told us that the climate change and global warming we are seeing now will happen,' he says. 'We continue to do our practices because we know they are correct – scientists are only just catching up with us now. For our children, we give them rich knowledge, a heritage, and resources. We don't worry about what will happen in the future. Try to save what you have. Show them how to save that.'

On a previous visit he had taken me to his home, sat me under a tree and fed me, introduced me to his youngest son. He showed me photos of his teenage daughter, studying at an English-medium school.

What he says now, about children, is not theoretical. It is a deeply held and personal belief.

'Covid was a warning that things are getting bad. The recent rains and the flash floods are unusual. We see things happening now, population pressures, pollution. It will lead to a situation like war, people will blame each other. India may go to Japan, for example, and say: "We are suffering from climate change because of fossil fuels but we didn't cause this problem," and Japan will say: "We don't care. It's not our problem." Countries will fight with each other. We see discussions and worry about the environment, but not action. World War Three will be fought on the environment, and our children will be the leaders, because they know about the environment.'

I am quietened, reflecting. A man brings up his children to care for the natural world around them. They absorb a deep, intimate knowledge of their environment. And yet this man is clear-headed enough to look forward ten years, twenty, maybe thirty. These Bishnoi villages are not just refuges: they are training grounds. Elsewhere, sooner than unite to take care of acute ecological pressures, the effects of climate change will drive people to war. Like the unarmed men who takes on armed poachers, like Amrita Devi and her daughters flinging their arms around a tree, Bishnoi children are being prepared for war. They are being brought up to alert us to what we should be fighting for.

We reach the shores of Jambhoji Lake, out near the village of Rurkali, and watch buffaloes enter the water. Their herders, brightly clothed Bishnoi ladies, stand on the bank. Buffaloes need watching. While cows don't get lost, a buffalo on the loose will just keep on walking. Six of the beasts in

the lake swim and swim, the calls of the ladies left far behind them. The women laugh and run along the bank to get ahead of them.

'How do you and the Tiger Force keep up your spirits?' I ask Ram Niwas. 'When you see all that is going wrong in the environment, do you sometimes lose hope?'

'Yes,' Ram Niwas admits. 'Sometimes, when we look at the crisis, at all the troubles we're facing, we get disheartened. Then somebody comes along and pays us a little attention and we feel better. We feel we are being heard.'

The lake is partly surrounded by a low wall that extends out from a temple complex. We enter through its main gate, past a temple being built for the monkey god Hanuman. The paving beyond the courtyard becomes crusted earth, and we reach an old and simple shrine. Two walls are open yet barred, the front is sealed by a gate, and to the rear is a blood-red wall. Here stands a portrait of Guru Jambhoji.

The gate is opened and Ram Niwas urges me inside. He sits on the left, I sit on the right. We fill the space and face Jambhoji.

There's an old tin on the black and white tiles, and Ram Niwas reaches in for a piece of coconut. It's coated in ghee. His first match sputters and dies, but a second flares and the coconut takes on the flame. With one piece of coconut he lights a second. The pieces burn from white to black and then to ash as Ram Niwas chants, his voice maintaining a loud, staggered rhythm while his hands clap offbeat. I join in with hand claps of my own.

I sense the meaning behind Ram Niwas's chanted words. He is sending up a prayer, that what I take away with me and write might carry the Bishnoi message to the world.

That it might be heard.

That people might help.

APPENDIX

The Twenty-nine Rules

THE TWENTY-NINE RULES made their first appearance in a poem by Udo Ji Nain, a disciple who encountered Jambhoji in the early years of the guru's teachings. I found my favourite version of these rules in Jajiwal Dhora, the Bishnoi temple where I first met flocks of feeding demoiselle cranes, on the outskirts of Jodhpur. They had been written by the temple's priest, Swami Bhagirath Das Acharya.

The first rule concerns childbirth. A mother must stay alone in a room with her baby for thirty days after giving birth. It's a time for mother and baby to rest and to bond. At the close of the thirtieth day, water blessed by a priest is given to mother and baby. With the taste of this water, known as *pahul*, the baby becomes a Bishnoi.

For five days after menstruating a woman must be spared any work. Then after a full bath her life resumes. That's the second rule, and the third states that everybody must wash themselves thoroughly first thing in the morning.

Rule four is to be modest and of good character. How, though? The answer is to note and stop any actions that bring feelings of shame. This should also prevent anyone married from being unfaithful. 'Control body, mind and human senses in order to turn the mind inward and realise our divine nature,' the priest's commentary suggests, with an illustration of a man and woman sitting cross-legged, slightly apart, meditating.

Be content, says rule four. Stay grateful and satisfied with what you have. You can still work hard to make progress in life and fulfil your dreams, but do that without being unhappy about what you lack. 'Keep the mountain top view,' suggests the priest, with things in perspective.

Stay clean in body and mind is rule six. This means washing with water but also 'meditation, right living, positive thinking and adopting the teachings of Sri Guru Jambhoji'.

Rules seven to nine concern religious practice. Meditate twice a day: dawn and dusk are the most conducive times. Sing praises to the Lord in the evening. And perform *havan* daily. This is the ritual in which ghee is offered to a flame, and scriptures and Jambhoji's teachings are recited.

The tenth rule is to filter water and milk, and brush insects off fuel before burning it. This protects insects, while filtering drinks also protects the health of the drinker.

The next rule is also to do with filtering: filter your speech. The priest gives Jambhoji's counsel on this. 'Speak truth, speak pleasingly. Don't speak unpleasantly though it is the truth and also don't speak falsehood, although it is pleasing.'

Rule twelve: be forgiving and compassionate. The temple's commentary points out that people who forgive and are compassionate are healthier and happier than those who hold on to resentment.

Thirteen is simple. Don't steal. Accepting a bribe is the equivalent of stealing.

Don't condemn others. Speaking ill of people when they are not there, being judgemental, is seen as a sign of mental illness.

Never tell a lie. The temple has a statement of Jambhoji's that takes this further: 'Speak the truth at all times: not just where it is convenient.'

Rule sixteen: Don't argue for the sake of arguing.

The day of a new moon, known as Amavasya, is especially auspicious. Rule seventeen is that people must fast on this day.

Rule eighteen: be kind to all living beings. This also requires no hunting or killing of animals. And the next rule extends this to 'green trees', ones with the sap still in them, that must not be cut down or trimmed for firewood.

Rule twenty: defeat your base passions. These are lust, pride, greed and delusional attachments.

Only eat food cooked by yourself or by someone leading a spiritual life, demands the next rule.

Rule twenty-two: give shelter to sheep and goats. The same goes for all animals in your care: the old ones are to be housed and fed till their natural death, not sent to slaughter. Similarly, shelter wounded or abandoned animals. And the next rule forbids the castration of bulls, because of the pain it causes them.

Four rules, twenty-four to twenty-seven, forbid the use of specific stimulants: opium, tobacco, cannabis and alcohol. (The rule against opium is openly flouted in some communities, and some Bishnoi villages are associated with the opium trade.)

Rule twenty-eight: be vegetarian. The eating of meat and eggs is forbidden.

The final rule is not to wear blue. That colour was drawn from use of the indigo bush, and so seen as destructive of the natural environment.

Woven through the temple's explanation of these rules is the constant urging to recite the name Vishnu. I have seen the rules arranged to make this a rule of its own.[66]

Other teachings are carried inside stories from Jambhoji's life. Here's one such:[67]

The setting is the sand dune of Samrathal Dhora, where Jambhoji made his home. Loha Pangal, a yogi and ascetic with long wild hair and a body smeared with ash, climbed up to confront him. This yogi lived a harsh ascetic life, had studied the sacred texts, and trained his mind so that it attained powers of physical force: he could make things appear and disappear, make them fly, he could fly himself.

The followers who climbed the hill with him had been hard won. They gave him his name, which translates as 'Iron-pants', because he wore underwear made of iron. And now Jambhoji with his new teachings was gaining the attention of all the spiritual seekers in the region. It was time to bring this upstart guru to heel. Loha Pangal challenged Jambhoji to combat by dialogue.

The visitor's opening salvo was a simple question. 'Where do you live?'

Jambhoji explained that he lived as pure existence, consciousness and bliss, in all realms and in formless space. 'I also live in all beings, inside and outside of them. Oh Loha Pangal! Once you know the supreme being, there is nothing more left to be known.'

From that lofty aspect, Jambhoji shifted to a critique. Loha Pangal had forgotten the true purpose of being born. It wasn't to sniff the dust of crematoria, to hobnob with disembodied spirits, or defile your body by smearing it with dust and ashes. Loha Pangal was no better than other yogis, ascetics or sanyasin who abandoned their daily lives to head out on a spiritual quest, nor the Brahmins, Islamic mullahs or scholars of sacred texts: all were narrow-minded, their sights blinkered by the tight bounds of their religion. 'Without the blessings of a competent guide,' Jambhoji told his visitor, 'all efforts go to waste.'

Loha Pangal's side of the dialogue involved asserting his occult powers and his bare-bones lifestyle. He was a supremely powerful yogi. Why couldn't Jambhoji admit that?

'Just by having a rich crop of dishevelled hair,' Jambhoji told him, 'and eating the flesh of innocent animals, you want to be called a yogi? Your mind keeps racing like an antelope. Keep it under control. Renounce ego, control your senses, then you'll be a yogi. Keep longing that everything is perfect, that you will have ever greater powers, that more and more people will praise your name, and you are stuck in bondage. Doing that, you are not a master, not a yogi, you are a slave. Please, Loha Pangal, do your best to understand. When you chase after belongings and fame, that's a sickness. You have to let them go to find what is real. Your mind is your worst enemy, but it's also your best friend. Make it free of all desires, even desire for freedom from the cycle of death and rebirth. Be absolutely desireless, live totally without ego, be humble like a lamb and you'll find you have no need to practise austerity or leave your home. That is real yoga.'

It was all very well for Jambhoji to say such things, but having attained his occult powers Loha Pangal found it hard to let them go. He needed Jambhoji to battle him on his own terms. 'If you are so powerful,' he said, 'then free me of my iron pants.'

'So be it.' And on the instant of Jambhoji speaking, the iron underwear turned to dust.

Loha Pangal, the master of occult powers, bent down before Jambhoji. From Jambhoji's hands he took *pahul*, water charged by the power of chanted mantras, and became a Bishnoi.

Endnotes

1. Nanditha Krishna, *Sacred Animals of India*, Penguin Books India, Gurgaon, 2010 (p.44). TheBishnoi population is estimated here at three and a quarter million. This figure comes from Patram Bishnoi, vice president of the Bishnoi Mahasabha, the religion's governing council. It is double what is recorded elsewhere, but came from a new survey and was presented as authoritative.

2. Several written sources state that Bishnois take the blackbuck as incarnations of Vishnu, and chinkara as incarnations of Jambhoji, but when I checked this with many Bishnois they all said this was nonsense. It was fine to take creatures as being sacred, but not to discriminate and say some are more sacred than others.

3. The actor was found guilty of the illegal killing of animals, as described by Rakesh Goswami in 'How Bishnois' compassion for wildlife led to Salman Khan's conviction in blackbuck poaching case', *Hindustan Times*, 6 April 2018.

The guilty verdict is under appeal, but while details are challenged the existence of the actors' hunting party in the village at this time is not seriously under dispute.

4. Press Trust of India, 'Chinkara Poaching Case', *NDTV.com*, 3 May 2016.

5. Harsha Kumari Singh, 'Make Salman Khan Surrender, Go Back To Jail: Rajasthan To Supreme Court', *NDTV.com*, 19 Oct 2016.

6. While it was admitted that the actors Saif Ali Khan, Sonali Bendre, Tabu and Neelam accompanied their co-star, they were acquitted of the killing: Harsha Kumari Singh, 'Salman Khan gets 5 years jail in 20-year-old blackbuck poaching case: a timeline', *NDTV.com*, 16 April 2018.

7. Details of the first postmortem can be found in this court report: Ajay Parmar and Swati Deshpande, 'Salman Khan: Blackbuck died of natural causes, not gunshot', *Times of India*, 28 Jan 2017.

8. Mohammed Iqbal, 'Reliable evidence against Salman led to sentencing', *The Hindu*, 6 April 2018.

9. The first postmortem was overturned by a second: Press Trust of India, 'Second Post-Mortem Report of Blackbucks Nailed Salman Khan', *NDTV.com*, 7 April 2018.

10. Gangadharan Menon, 'The Land of The Bishnois – Where Conservation of Wildlife Is A Religion!' *The Better India*, 3 July 2012.

11. Maninder Dabas, 'Here's How DNA Identification Sealed the Fate of Salman Khan in Blackbuck Poaching Case', *India Times*, 6 April 2018.

12. Rakesh Goswami, 'How Bishnois' compassion for wildlife led to Salman Khan's conviction in blackbuck poaching case', *Hindustan Times*, 6 April 2018.

13. For a simple guide to the decades-long legal fight, see: 'A Timeline of the Blackbuck Killing Case', *Economic Times*, 7 May 2018.

14. Shashank Bengali, 'Global Development: This nature-loving sect in India dragged one of the world's biggest movie stars to court – and won', *The Los Angeles Times*, 17 May 2018.

15. *Economic Times*, 7 May 2018 (as endnote 13).

16. Maninder Dabas, 'Bishnois & 20 Years of Struggle: Here's How The Community's Love For Blackbuck Led To Salman Khan's Conviction', *India Times*, 6 April 2018.

17. Bobby Luthra Sinha and Anand Singh, 'Embodying a Preparedness to Die: Why Bishnois of Western Rajasthan Rise in Defence of the Blackbuck and the Chinkara?' *Sociological Bulletin*, vol. 69, issue 1, 5 Feb 2020 (p.42).

18. Maninder Dabas, 'Bishnois & 20 Years of Struggle', *India Times*, 6 April 2018.

19. *Economic Times*, 7 May 2018 (as endnote 13).

20. The intense scrutiny of the driver is shown in post-trial when he is reported as seeking police protection: Press Trust of India, 'Salman Khan Poaching Case: Key Witness Demands Police Protection', *India.com*, 29 July 2016.

21. This article recounts the UK's rejection of a visa for the actor, on account of his conviction, and cites several related cases in which Khan has been charged: Gitanjali Roy, 'Salman Khan's UK Visa Rejected Due to Conviction in Poaching Cases', *NDTV.com*, 2 Aug 2013.

22. 'Salman Khan gets exemption from appearance in blackbuck poaching case hearing after counsel cites COVID risk', *Economic Times*, 1 Dec 2020.

23. Michael Safi, 'Bollywood star Salman Khan sentenced to five years for killing antelopes', *The Guardian*, 5 April 2018.

24. For more details of this 2022 cell-block interview, see: Aishwarya Ragupati, 'All shocking confessions made by Lawrence Bishnoi against Salman Khan', *NewsBytes*, 14 July 2022.

25. Grace Cyril, 'After getting gun licence, Salman Khan spotted in bulletproof Toyota Land Cruiser SUV worth Rs 1.5 crore', *India Today*, 2 Aug 2022.

26. Mihir Bave, 'Bollywood Actor Salman Khan Brings Home Bulletproof Nissan Patrol SUV', *Car and Bike*, 12 April 2023.

27. Princia Hendriques, 'Salman Khan confirms he was sleeping when Bishnoi gang members fired at home', *Mashable India*, 13 June 2024.

28. Devesh Kumar, '"Salman Khan should come to our temple and...": Bishnoi community head open to consider apology in blackbuck case', *Mint*, 14 May 2024.

29. Dialogue from Teenaa Kaur Pasrichan, *The Deer, Tree and Me*, Films Division of India, 2020.

30. An excerpt from *Sangoshti Vaani*, a Bishnoi conservation journal, quoted in Herma Brockmann and Renato Pichler, *Paving the Way for Peace*, Delhi, Low Price Publications, 2004 (p.63–7).

31. Brockmann and Pichler (as above), p.65.

32. Sachin Saini, '17-year-old Rajasthan boy fought with armed chinkara poachers, chased them', *Hindustan Times*, 13 May 2020.

33. A tale from later in Jambhoji's life reflects on this incident. One of his followers was distraught, because her son had grown old enough to speak but would not do so. She consulted doctors, astrologers, spiritual people, and they told her about her son's former life. He had been a great yogi, but due to some sexual escapade he had been reborn into a simple life as her son. The great yogi's practice of maintaining silence had stuck with the boy.

Come sit beside me, Jambhoji said to the boy. Normally, as the writer M.S. Chanda suggests, Jambhoji refrained from using occult powers. 'He wanted his followers to follow a normal, healthy life, relying upon their intelligence and intellect, doing hard work, with faith in one God, Vishnu.' But Jambhoji had been through his own trauma of reincarnation, squeezed from boundless spiritual experience into the human frame of baby then boy, and so recognised that this silent boy beside him was not just one of his followers. He drew the boy into a shared meditative state, softly clicked his fingers, and then posed a question. Addressing the boy as the 'self-born lord of the universe' he asked, 'What made you leave your heavenly abode and come down to the earth? For what great purpose have you taken birth, free from all desires, beyond sensual pleasure, immersed in meditation, lit with divine light? You are the light manifest.'

Knowing himself to be understood, the boy responded. He gave Jambhoji details of the childhood of his previous life, his growth as an adult, and becoming a powerful yogi. Jambhoji had said he was beyond sensual pleasure. Well, that wasn't always so. In that last life, he had succumbed to sexual desire. Since then he had spent a great deal of time in superior plains before being ready to be born into a good family.

His mother heard these details of her son's former life, and his experiences in spiritual realms, but they meant nothing to her. She sat and watched her boy's mouth move, and a stream of coherent sentences emerge from his lips. Her boy could speak! She bowed to Jambhoji, gave him great thanks, and walked with her son back into family life.

34. University Of Arkansas, 'Researchers Find Evidence Of 16th Century Epic Drought Over North America', *Science Daily*, 8 Feb 2000.

35. John Last, 'This Summer's Drought Is Europe's Worst in 500 Years. What Happened Last Time?' *Smithsonian Magazine*, 8 Sept 2022.

36. Thomas Blade, 'Europe's drought could be the worst 500 years, warns researcher', *Euronews*, 10 Aug 2022.

37. 'Europe's droughts since 2015 "worst in 2,000 years"', *France 24*, 15 Feb 2021.

38. Om Prakash Bishnoi, Director of Jai Narain Vyas University's Jambhoji Research Institute, states that Jambhoji 'found a simple way of teaching science and conservation principles to his followers, who were mostly rural, uneducated and farmers, by incorporating them into religion. He knew beforehand that for the simple, god-fearing people, this was the only way to learn and remember.' Quoted in Payal Mago, Reena Bhatiya, Nupur Gosain and Deekshant Awasthi, 'Bishnoi community model: an Indian Ecological Feminist approach to environment protection', *Ecofeminism and Climate Change*, vol. 3, issue 1, May 2022.

39. Though commentators separate the rules into thirds, governing relations with the natural world, human behaviour, and spiritual practice, they are meant to be taken as a whole and not divided in this way. Take the example of Amrita Devi. She could not let a living tree be felled, but nor would she give a bribe which she understood would be as bad as

stealing, and her actions were in accord with and shaped by her religious beliefs and practices. Caring for nature is an integral part of human behaviour and of the spiritual life.

40. During her encounters with the Bishnoi, Alexis Reichert was told of a different transaction. 'Villagers said "we cannot take free food, we must work for it". "OK," he [Jambhoji] said, "then take the sand from the bottom and carry it to the top," he explained that this way, ponds will be created at the bottom for water and God will give grains at the top of the dunes.' This practice is still in evidence at Samrathal Dhora, where pilgrims carry sand up to the top of the sacred dune, and a pond has been created at the bottom. The tale comes from Alexis Reichert's MA thesis: 'Sacred Trees, Sacred Deer, Sacred Duty to Protect: Exploring Relationships between Humans and Nonhumans in the Bishnoi Community', University of Ottawa, 2015 (p.37).

41. While Hindus cremate their dead, the Bishnoi opt for burial. The wood from trees is too precious to burn for cremation. Sacred words of Jambhoji are recited for the dead body to hear and it is washed and dressed in cotton clothes, white for men and red for women. Soon after the following sunrise, barefoot male relatives carry the body to the burial ground. With the

head facing north, it is laid in a grave that is three feet deep and the mourners drop in sand till the body is covered. Back home from the ceremony, the relatives prepare the deceased's favourite food and feed it to crows; through them the food is thought to reach the departed. A portion of the sweets fed to guests is offered to a fire and then mixed with yoghurt and taken to the burial ground. As a final farewell, water is poured onto a khejri tree through a woollen cloth containing grain. A small group of mourners then peels away to perform final rituals by the banks of the Ganges.

42. Founded in 1982, the Institute is part of the Ministry of Environment, Forest and Climate Change but has its own autonomy. Its focus is on field research that develops wildlife science, which it then applies to conservation.

43. The pandemic brought a pause to those annual surveys, but in places where chinkara were free-roaming and abundant on my 2020 visit, I saw none two years later.

44. Jovita Aranha, 'This Roadside Mechanic from Rajasthan has rescued over 1,180 injured wild animals!', The Better India, 18 Dec 2018.

45. Payal Mago, Reena Bhatiya, Nupur Gosain, and Deekshant Awasthi, 'Bishnoi community model: an Indian

Ecological Feminist approach to environment protection', *Ecofeminism and Climate Change*, vol.3, issue 1, May 2022.

46. I queried whether these rules on strict segregation of women, particularly during the menstrual cycle, was more to do with regarding women as impure in this period, as happens in some traditional societies where isolation is to prevent supposed contamination. It was more about women getting a chance to rest and eat well, a group of women assured me. And the segregation after birth is so a child doesn't pick up any infections. Yes, there was also the contamination element, but: 'There were no sanitary pads back then,' Vijay Laxmi explains. 'Things could get messy.'

Patram Bishnoi, vice president of the Bishnoi Mahasabha but a man of independent opinion, brought in a practical viewpoint. 'Tell the men the women need rest and to be taken care of, and they might just say forget it, let them work,' he says. 'Tell them "she's impure" and ...' he makes the gesture of casting them to one side with his hand, 'they'll make sure the woman does no work and gets some rest.'

47. Pankaj Jain notes how he was told that the covering was once of green rather than saffron cloth, suggesting Jambhoji's connection to the Sufi movement, the switch in colour happening after the partition between India and Pakistan, but all his respondents on site denied this.

48. Inder Pal Bishnoi, *Vishnoi from Vishnu*, Lucknow, BFC Publications, 2021 (p.160).

49. Prof. Vinay Kumar Srivastava's notes on his encounters with the Bishnoi are from his article, 'Religion and Environment: a perspective from the community of the Bishnois', in Sukant K. Chaudhury (ed.), *Culture, Ecology and Sustainable Development*, New Delhi, Mittal Publications, 2006 (p.204).

50. 'Amrita Devi inspired Gaura Devi to lead a band of intrepid women', *The Hindu*, 14 April 2011. Pankaj Jain, a pre-eminent English-language scholar of the Bishnois, discusses how Chipko leaders trace the movement's origins to the Khejarli martyrs in a filmed discussion, 'Dr. Pankaj Jain chats with Sahana Singh on Bishnois and Indic Environmentalism', *Indica Today*, 13 April 2018.

51. Jyoti Thakur, '50 Years On, Vimla Bahuguna on the Chipko Movement, her late husband and ties that bind', *Article 14.com*, 1 March 2023.

52. Shekhar Pathak, *The Chipko Movement: A People's History*, New Delhi, Permanent Black, 2021 (p.132).

53. Ishan Kukreti, '"Greed will consume the village": Chipko

birthplace questions its choice after Chamoli disaster', *Down to Earth*, 17 Feb 2021.

54. India Development Review, 'In Conversation with Dr Vandana Shiva,' *Feminism in India*, 15 Oct 2029.

55. Vandana Shiva, *Oneness vs. the 1%: Shattering Illusions, Seeding Freedom*, London, Chelsea Green, 2020 (p.15).

56. Pankaj Jain, *Dharma and Ecology of Hindu Communities*, London, Ashgate, 2011 (p.71).

57. Harsh Vardhan, 'Bishnoi Fascination', in Brockman and Pichler (see endnote 30).

58. This is why no bustard, for example, now flies unnoticed into power lines. From his small desert village Radheshyam takes it as his immediate duty to issue a press release: 'Another Great Indian Bustard dies after hitting high-tension wires.'

59. 'Brutalized for resistance,' ed. Jo Woodman, Survival International, 2022.

60. Seema Mundoli, 'How a tree-hugging protest transformed Indian environmentalism', *Nature* 627, 26 March 2024 (p.732).

61. Alok Prakash Putul, 'In the midst of coal shortage reports, a coal mine extension is approved in pristine Hasdeo forests', *Mongabay*, 25 May 2022.

62. Gerry Shih, Karishma Mehrotra and Anant Gupta, 'India cracks down on critics of coal', *Washington Post*, 5 June 2023,

63. Nikhil Inamdar, 'Adani Group: Chhattisgarh tribes' year-long protest against tycoon's coal mine', *BBC News*, 20 March 2023.

64. Introduction to Aidan Rankin, *The Jain Path*, O Books, Winchester, UK, 2006 (p.xiv). As part of the scholarly debate, C.H. Chapple argues that while Jain philosophy can be seen to 'approximate an environmentally friendly ideal', the primary Jain focus is 'on personal, spiritual advancement, not on a holistic vision of interrelatedness of life' (C.H. Chapple, ed., *Jainism and ecology: Nonviolence in the web of life*, Motilal Banarsidass, Delhi, 2006, p.138). In an essay in the same volume ('Green Jainism? Notes and queries toward a possible Jain environmental ethic', p.65), J.E. Cort saw 'no Jain environmental ethic per se' and that statements which suggest that 'Jainism has always "enthroned the philosophy of ecological harmony" are largely untrue as statements about history'.

65. The Vedas give us the accounts of the first nine incarnations of Vishnu, Krishna being the ninth, and a leading yet sceptical Bishnoi I met with insisted it stopped there. While he was a devotee of Jambhoji, chanting his words each morning, he saw Jambhoji

as an exemplar of what a man could achieve through devotion, chanting and meditation.

Many Hindus accept that Lord Venkateshwara, in his appearance subsequent to the Vedas, was the tenth incarnation of Vishnu, his hilltop temple in Tirupati being the most prosperous in India from the money donated by crowds of pilgrims. This would make Jambhoji the eleventh such incarnation. While Jambhoji's teachings recorded in the *shabads* sometimes differentiate between the man and the divine voice he accesses, for example 'This is my supernatural voice that does not remember born creatures', he is also quite clear about the divine nature of his incarnation, on Earth to free a specified number of souls.

66. Several versions of the Vishnu chant are offered in Inder Pal Bishnoi's *Vishnoi from Vishnu*, Lucknow, BFC Publications, 2021 (p.64–7). The first is 'Om Vishnu', with Om (pronounced aa-oo-m) understood as a primal sound that pre-existed the creation of the universe. In this book, Inder Pal Bishnoi makes the case that Bishnois should be called Vishnois, worshippers of Vishnu, with this silent chanting of the Vishnu mantra their principal concern. 'If one repeats mantras with deep love and longing in silence, one can build a communion with the Supreme Being.'

67. Taken and adapted from M.S. Chandla, *Jambhoji, Messiah of the Thar Desert*, Chandigarh, Aurva Publications, 1998.

Photos

p.122 In her house, a Bishnoi woman pours ghee on a *havan* while praying to Guru Jambhoji. Lohawat, Rajasthan. *Franck Vogel*

p.134–5 Rakesh Bishnoi, aged twelve, looks after the family buffaloes. Dhawa Dolli, Rajasthan. *Franck Vogel*

p.142 Ranaram Bishnoi, the 'tree man', back from his morning's work near his home at Ekalkhori, Rajasthan. *Martin Goodman*

p.150–51 Ranaram Bishnoi and his camel crossing the desert to bring water to the trees he has planted. *Franck Vogel*

p.156 A Bishnoi woman waters a tree in her courtyard near Abohar in Punjab. *Franck Vogel*

p.164 Devangini Bishnoi and her street dogs, Jaipur. *Martin Goodman*

p.172 The illegally felled khejri trees unearthed from the trenches in which they were buried, in the solar fields between the cities of Bikaner and Phalodi, Rajasthan, 2022. *Martin Goodman*

p.182 Chipko movement women hugging a tree, Uttar Pradesh, 1982. *Bhawan Singh/The India Today Group via Getty Images*

p.188–9 A Bishnoi woman collecting fresh cow pats to dry in the sun and use for fuel, Lohawat, Rajasthan. *Franck Vogel*

p.194 A Bishnoi woman breastfeeding her child and a chinkara. *Vijay Bedi*

p.204 Lalu Ram Bishnoi brings an orphan fawn near the chinkara herd to try to find it a stepmother. *Franck Vogel*

p.208–9 Members of the Tiger Force guarding evidence as they wait for the police near a dead chinkara which was killed by poachers and thrown out from the car while the Bishnois were in pursuit, 2008. *Franck Vogel*

p,214 Guru Jambhoji transmitting the light of succession to Vilhoji. From a painting in Vilhoji's shrine at the temple in Ramrawas Kalan, Rajasthan. *Martin Goodman*

p.218–9 Ranaram Bishnoi, who as well as planting trees spreads grain each morning and evening for the chinkara and birds near his home. *Franck Vogel*

p.224 Bishnoi schoolchildren in the village of Dhawa Doli, near Jodhpur. *Martin Goodman*

p.234–5 Rakesh Bishnoi riding the backs of the family's buffaloes while they bathe. Dhawa Doli, Rajasthan. *Franck Vogel*

p.238 A portrait of Guru Jambhoji at the hilltop shrine near Rotu, Rajasthan. *Martin Goodman*

p.246–7 Vishudha Nand, a Bishnoi priest, performing *havan* at Jajiwal Dhora, Rajasthan. *Franck Vogel*

Thanks

MY DEEP THANKS to the Bishnoi community – and especially to those whose stories are shared here – for welcoming me into their lives and homes.

Harsh Vardhan listened to me, a stranger, saw what I needed, and connected me to the Bishnoi. He stayed attentive throughout my journeys and is utterly instrumental in this book's coming into being. He is a a peerless conservationist and a fine photographer too, and I am glad to have his portrait of Ram Niwas Bishnoi Budhnagar grace the book.

Vijay Laxmi Bishnoi orchestrated my second journey, opening her network of friends, colleagues and acquaintances, and much of the kind attention I received was due to a natural reverence and respect people feel for her. I was treated to many meals along the way, in homes and temples, everyone alerted to my needs for a gluten-free diet.

Ganpat Bishnoi volunteered exceptional help as a translator and guide. Much of the trust I was shown was due to the trust people felt in him, and he too opened my way to people and stories found here. We shared a fine adventure.

Rohit Jindal kindly acted as my translator for the last days of my stay, and shared his research from field trips to the Bishnoi *orans*.

The brothers Ram Niwas Bishnoi and Narendra Bishnoi were exceptionally welcoming and helpful, perfect exemplars of all that Bishnois can be. Ram Niwas first saw the need for this book and shepherded it into being. I am grateful for his generous preface.

Nobody in the west has done more than Peter Wohlleben to heighten our knowledge and appreciation of trees, and I am very touched that the book now includes his clear-eyed and heartfelt foreword.

Moolaram Vishnoi gave me copies of his helpful and original research, and his own copy of an irreplaceable book, Prithwi Raj Bishnoi's *Guru Shri Jambhoji and Sabadvaani* (Jambhani Sahitya Academy, Bikaner, 2018).

Patram Bishnoi opened his home for my stay in Rotu, and along with his wife Dimple Bishnoi hosted me for a meeting with some remarkable women in his Jodhpur home.

Rajaram Bishnoi came from his home in Bikaner to show me sacred sites and temples around the town of Jangloo, a happy visit that deeply informed my stay; its account will appear on my website, with other material from which I learned a good deal but which did not slip into this book.

Pankaj Jain's *Dharma and Ecology of Hindu Communities* (Ashgate, Oxford, 2016) includes a great deal of research drawn from his time among the Bishnoi and the book has been a wise and constant companion. His translation of the *shabads*, along with Prithwi Raj Bishnoi's, is the source of most of Jambhoji's sayings quoted through the book.

M.S. Chandla's *Jambhoji, Messiah of the Thar Desert* (Aurva Publications, Chandigarh, 1998), read with thanks to the British Library, gave most fuel to Jambhoji's life stories.

My thanks go also to James Thornton, for being my rock and the perfect first reader.

Mark Ellingham for Profile, and the team of Rob Sanders, Jen Gauthier and Paula Ayer at Greystone, took on stewardship of this book and helped to guide it into the shape you find here.

That shape prospered with the fine page design of Henry Iles, Susanne Hillen's proofreading, and Bill Johncocks bringing his magic to the index. Mark soared way beyond regular editorial duties in turning this book into the handsome illustrated edition it has become.

Franck Vogel is a true champion of the Bishnois and their philosophy, and it is a great honour to have his magnificent photographs featured throughout this book. Radheshyam Pemani Bishnoi showed me the Great Indian Bustards and has given the book one of his terrific photos, complemented by the telling bustard photo by Dr Devesh Ghadavi.

My thanks to the Society of Authors and the Authors' Foundation whose award helped me to finance this book.

Patrick Walsh first encouraged this book when it was a germ of an idea out in Jaipur and has been perfectly assiduous in his support in the years since. He is an agent with his own mission to save the planet; his extensive notes on multiple drafts and his belief in what this book has to offer kept it going.

And the last word to Guru Jambhoji, whose life and teachings have fruited so well in generations of Bishnoi.

Index

Note: Page references in italics indicate photographs. The suffix 'n' refers to a footnote and 'n' followed by a number to an endnote (see pp. 249–56).

P

pahul (initiation) 221, 239, 244
Pandey, Devendra 103
Pangal, Loha 242–4
Pathak, Shakhar 191, **254n52**
patients, tree planting 162
peafowl 36, 79, 119, 121, 136, 157, 168
pesticides 120, 226–7
pests, shoot borer beetle 132–3
Phitkasni village and temple 157–9
pilgrims *16–17, 86–7, 1*36, 221, **253n40**
Pipasar, birthplace of Guru Jambhoji 71–2, 77–8
ploughing as men's work 184
poaching 55, 98, 195, 210, 216
  see also hunting
police action against protesters 199
Poonamchand (witness to illegal hunting) 41–4
powerlines, bird strikes on 96–7, 105–8
Prakash, Om 211
Pramod (son of Prasan Goswami) 226
prayer from Ram Niwas 236–7
priesthood, Bishnoi 52, 58–9, 140, 216–17, 246–7
Prince Jaisal 99
Prince Rao Duda 77–8, 131, 140–1
Pushpa (wife to Shaitan) 55–7
Pyush (Shaitan's son) 55, 57–8, 60

R

Rajasthan
  as a Bishnoi holy land 77
  chief veterinary officer 42
  chief wildlife warden 109
  chinkara population 127
  heatwaves 81, 84–5
  human population 168
  state bird 95
  state tree 178
Rajasthan High Court 198
Rajendarand, Swami 91
Rajendranatha, Yogi 74
Raksha, 'Voice of the Voiceless' 104
Ram Niwas *see* Bishnoi, Ram Niwas
Ramanand-ji 139, 141
Ramayana, the 29
Ramesh, Jairan 183
Ramrawas Kalan (village) *214*, 215, 217, 222
Rana, Asha Devi 192
Rana, Chandra Singh (Gaura Devi's son) 185–6, 192
Ranaram ('the Tree man') *see* Bishnoi, Ranaram
Rao Duda Jodhawat Rathod, Prince 77–8, 131, 140–1
Red List, United Nations 35
  see also endangered species
reflectors on powerlines 97
religion, founders of
  retreats 80
  stemming from other religions 139
Reni forest sale, 1973 185
Reni (village) 184–6, 190
retreats, of religions' founders 80
Ridmil, Rao 158
ring-road campaign 205–6, 225
Rishiganga Hydroelectric Project 191
road accidents 67, 115–16, 166–7
rohida tree (*Tecomella undulata*) 145
Rotu temple 129–31, 136, 238
Royal Bank of Scotland 119
rules of Bishnoism *see* twenty-nine rules